GOOD OLD-FASHIONED
COMFORT
PUDDINGS

GOOD OLD-FASHIONED
COMFORT
PUDDINGS

Sara Paston-Williams

National Trust

First published in the United Kingdom in 2010 by
National Trust Books
10 Southcombe Street
London
W14 0RA

An imprint of Anova Books Company Ltd

Recipes sourced from *Good Old-Fashioned Puddings*, published by National Trust Books 2007

ISBN: 9781905400911

A CIP catalogue record for this book is available from the British Library.

18 17 16 15 14 13 12 10
10 9 8 7 6 5 4 3 2 1

Reproduction by Dot Gradations Ltd, UK
Printed by Toppan Leefung Printing Ltd, China

This book can be ordered direct from the publisher at the website www.anovabooks.com,
or try your local bookshop. Also available at National Trust shops and www.nationaltrustbooks.co.uk.

CONTENTS

INTRODUCTION

Blessed be he that invented pudding! For it is manna that hits the palates of all sorts of people, better even than that of the wilderness. Ah! what an excellent thing is an English pudding! To come in pudding-time is as much as to say to come in the most lucky moment in the world.

This was written by Monsieur Misson de Valbourg, a French visitor to Britain in 1690. Another visitor, an Italian, around the same time wrote home saying 'English pies and puddings are literally stuffed with dried fruits and no-one who has not seen it with his own eyes could possibly believe what an incredible number of such pies and puddings the average Englishman is capable of eating!'

The British tradition for delicious puddings is centuries old. Puddings – pies, trifles, fools, flummeries, betties and tarts – have all been served regularly since medieval times. From the earliest recipes, through elaborate Elizabethan and Stuart confections to the elegant 18th- and substantial 19th-century puddings, a tradition has evolved which is an integral part of Britain's culinary heritage.

Almost all British puddings (and here, as in the rest of the book, I am using the word to describe any dish served at the sweet course) have descended from two medieval dishes: the early cereal 'pottage', which was a kind of porridge with honey, wild fruits, shredded meat or fish added to make it more palatable, and 'frumenty', a milk pudding made from wheat or barley and eaten with milk and honey on festive occasions.

Originally, puddings such as brightly coloured spiced jellies, flummeries, syllabubs, various tarts, custards, junkets and fruit dishes formed part of a second or third course of a meal, served alongside chicken and fish dishes. A typical second course might consist of veal, sweetbreads, lobster, apricot tart and, in the middle of the table, a pyramid of syllabubs and jellies. In Tudor and Stuart times a special course of sweetmeats known as a 'banquet' became fashionable among the rich.

The enormous variety of puddings and the rapidity with which they were developed in the 17th and 18th centuries, as sugar became cheaper and more available to everyone, show that they filled a real need in the British people's diet – rich in fat and carbohydrates to keep out the cold, and in sugar and fruit to build up energy. The puddings of country folk were often made from meal of cheaper local grains such as oats and barley rather than wheat, but they were just as satisfying.

British cooking has always been influenced by its monarchs and our puddings are no exception. Elizabeth I received annually 'a great pye of quinces, oringed' from her master of the pastry at New Year celebrations. George I was known as 'Pudding George' and is probably the Georgie Porgie mentioned in the well-known nursery rhyme. He, followed by George II and III, loved fattening, suety boiled puddings and dumplings which were devoured all over the kingdom. It was also quite common to see plum duffs and currant dumplings being sold in London streets for a halfpenny each.

With the French Revolution came a great transformation in British cooking. Many French chefs fled to Britain and a change of fashion in court circles resulted in the vogue for employing them. Antonin Carême, who worked for the Emperor Napoleon, was lured to Britain to work for the Prince Regent. Queen Victoria employed a number of French chefs, the most famous being Francatelli, who created puddings which we still know – Queen's Pudding, Her Majesty's Pudding, Empress Pudding and Albert Pudding. This fashion was soon copied by a growing and increasingly prosperous middle class who, socially aspiring, encouraged their cooks to make French dishes or, failing that, simply to give French names to traditional British ones. Many of the most delicious and subtle puddings of Georgian times were temporarily forgotten, giving way to rather heavy nursery-style puddings influenced by the German taste of Prince Albert.

Growing literacy had a tremendous influence on cookery. It allowed people, especially women, to write down their favourite recipes, including regional dishes. Many of the traditional pudding recipes were preserved in rural areas, particularly in the large country houses. In towns, speciality restaurants, gentlemen's clubs and the grill rooms of the more exclusive hotels continued to serve truly British puddings, so that many recipes have survived, although not always in their original form. In recent years, British food has enjoyed a well-deserved revival, with more and more hotels and restaurants serving our great national dishes and regional specialities. Puddings are a great attraction. Although some are inclined to be rich and fattening, they are homely and delicious and make a lovely treat. Despite our modern obsession with calories, 'pudding-time' still brings murmurs of delight from guests as they tuck into a syrup sponge or plum crumble. Our traditional puddings are glorious – rich and indulgent and comforting. Naughty? Yes, but oh so nice!

NOTE:

If you want to be a little less indulgent, yoghurt and crème fraîche can be used instead of cream in most recipes, or half and half.

VEGETARIAN ALTERNATIVES:

Vegetarian suet and the vegetarian equivalent of lard can be used wherever a recipe includes suet or lard in its ingredients. In fact, I prefer to use vegetarian suet as it gives a lighter finish. Vegetarian setting agents can also be used in place of gelatine, though you must always follow the manufacturer's instructions closely.

CONVERSIONS

Weight	Liquid measure	Length	Temperature
15g (½oz)	15ml (½fl oz)	5mm (¼in)	110°C, 225°F, gas mark ¼
25g (1oz)	30ml (1fl oz)	1cm (½in)	120°C, 250°F, gas mark ½
40g (1½oz)	50ml (2fl oz)	1.5cm (⅝in)	140°C, 275°F, gas mark 1
55g (2oz)	75ml (2½fl oz)	2cm (¾in)	150°C, 300°F, gas mark 2
70g (2½oz)	100ml (3½fl oz)	2.5cm (1in)	160°C, 325°F, gas mark 3
85g (3oz)	125ml (4fl oz)	5cm (2in)	180°C, 350°F, gas mark 4
100g (3½oz)	150ml (5fl oz or ¼ pint)	7cm (2¾in)	190°C, 375°F, gas mark 5
115g (4oz)	200ml (7fl oz or ½ pint)	9cm (3½in)	200°C, 400°F, gas mark 6
125g (4½oz)	250ml (9fl oz)	10cm (4in)	220°C, 425°F, gas mark 7
140g (5oz)	300ml (10fl oz or ½ pint)	13cm (5in)	230°C, 450°F, gas mark 8
150g (5½oz)	350ml (12fl oz)	15cm (6in)	240°C, 475°F, gas mark 9
175g (6oz)	400ml (14fl oz)	18cm (7in)	
200g (7oz)	425ml (15fl oz or ¾ pint)	20cm (8in)	
225g (8oz)	500ml (18fl oz)	23cm (9in)	
250g (9oz)	600ml (20fl oz or 1 pint)	25cm (10in)	
300g (10½oz)		28cm (11in)	
350g (12oz)		30cm (12in)	
375g (13oz)			
400g (14oz)			
425g (15oz)			
450g (1lb)			
675g (1½lb)			
900g (2lb)			

AMERICAN EQUIVALENTS

Dry measures

I US cup	50g (¾oz)	breadcrumbs; cake crumbs
I US cup	85g (3oz)	porridge or rolled oats
I US cup	90g (3¼oz)	ground almonds; shredded coconut
I US cup	100g (3½oz)	roughly chopped walnuts and other nuts; icing sugar; cocoa; drinking chocolate; flaked almonds; grated Cheddar cheese
I US cup	150g (5½oz)	white flour; currants; rice flour; muesli; cornflour; chopped dates
I US cup	175g (6oz)	wholemeal flour; oatmeal; raisins; sultanas; dried apricots; mixed candied peel
I US cup	200g (7oz)	caster sugar; soft brown sugar; demerara sugar; rice; glacé cherries; semolina; chopped figs or plums
I US cup	225g (8oz)	granulated sugar; curd cheese; cream cheese
I US cup	300g (10½oz)	mincemeat; marmalade; jam
I US cup	350g (12oz)	golden syrup; black treacle

Liquid measures

⅛ US cup	30ml (1fl oz)	
¼ US cup	50ml (2fl oz)	
½ US cup	125ml (4fl oz)	
I US cup	250ml (9fl oz)	
1¼ US cups	300ml (10fl oz)	
1¾ US cups	425ml (15fl oz)	
2 US cups	500ml (18fl oz)	
2½ US cups	600ml (20fl oz)	

Measures for fats

¼ stick	25g (1oz)	
I stick	100g (3½oz)	
(½ US cup)		

PASTRY RECIPES

SHORTCRUST PASTRY

450g (1lb) plain flour, sifted
A pinch of salt
100g (4oz) butter, softened
100g (4oz) lard, softened
3–4 tablespoons cold water

Mix together the flour and salt. Cut the fats into small pieces and rub into the flour until the mixture resembles fine breadcrumbs. Gradually add enough water, mixing with a fork, to give a stiff, but pliable dough. Knead lightly for a few minutes until smooth. Wrap in clingfilm or a plastic bag and chill for at least 15 minutes before using.

PUFF PASTRY

450g (1lb) plain flour, sifted
1 teaspoon salt
450g (1lb) butter, softened
1 teaspoon lemon juice
75–100ml (3–4fl oz) iced water

Mix together the flour and salt. Add 50g (2oz) of the butter, cut into small pieces, and rub into the flour until the mixture resembles fine breadcrumbs. Add the lemon juice and enough water to give a soft dough, similar to the consistency of butter. Knead lightly until really smooth. In a clean linen cloth, shape the remaining butter into a rectangle. On a lightly floured board, roll out the pastry to a rectangle slightly wider than the rectangle of butter and about twice its length. Place the butter on one half of the pastry and fold the other half over. Press the edges together with a rolling pin. Leave in a cool place for 15 minutes to allow the butter to harden slightly. Roll out the pastry to a long strip three times its original length, but keeping the width the same. The corners should be square, the sides straight and the thickness even. The butter must not break through the dough. Fold the bottom third up and the top third down, press the edges together with a rolling pin, put inside a well-oiled plastic bag and chill for 30 minutes. Place the dough on the floured board with the folded edges to your right and left, and roll out into a long strip as before. Fold again into three and chill for a further 30 minutes. Repeat this process four times more and chill for 30 minutes before using.

This is best made over two days, rolling three times and chilling overnight before completing the rolling the following day.

BAKED PUDDINGS

The discovery of the pudding cloth in the 17th century was a vital factor in the great expansion of pudding-eating, but Elizabethan cooks had already devised another method of cooking puddings that avoided boiling in animal guts. The pudding mixture was baked in a 'coffyn' or 'platter' in the bread or side oven with a pastry crust over it like a tart. In the early part of the 17th century, a pudding baked in a pot was still known as a 'pudding pye'. Occasionally the baking dish was lined with a thin sheet of pastry before the pudding mixture went into it, though this practice became more frequent in the 18th century. Sometimes the pastry was simply used to garnish the brim of the baking dish, to make it look elegant enough to be brought straight from the oven to the table.

Soon recipes for baked puddings were appearing regularly in cookery books. They were often based upon rich ingredients and this, together with the fact that an oven had to be heated for their baking, made them dishes for the wealthy rather than the poor. Fresh fruits in season were often substituted for the dried 'plums' in many recipes and baked puddings containing apples, apricots, Seville oranges, lemons and even carrots were common. Specially turned wooden baking dishes were sold in which the puddings could be cooked.

To give a crisp surface, a baked pudding mixture should be slightly softer than for a steamed or boiled pudding. If you use water instead of milk to soften the mixture, you will make a lighter pudding. To prevent jam, marmalade or chocolate from caramelizing during baking, stand your baking dish in a roasting tin half-filled with water.

APPLE DAPPY

A traditional Victorian recipe from the West Country, where apples were grown in vast quantities both for eating and for cider-making.

FOR THE LEMON SYRUP
1 large lemon
1 tablespoon golden syrup
15g (½oz) butter
115g (4oz) caster sugar
200ml (7fl oz) water

FOR THE PUDDING
225g (8oz) self-raising flour
1 level teaspoon baking powder
55g (2oz) butter, cut in pieces
150ml (¼ pint) milk
450g (1lb) cooking apples
1 tablespoon demerara sugar
½ teaspoon ground cinnamon
   or allspice

Serves 4–6

Preheat the oven to 190°C, 375°F, gas mark 5.

To make the lemon syrup, peel the lemon as thinly as possible and squeeze out the juice. Place the lemon rind, juice and all the other ingredients into a pan and heat gently, stirring until the sugar is dissolved. Leave to stand until needed.

Sieve the flour and baking powder into a large mixing bowl and rub in the butter until the mixture resembles breadcrumbs. Mix to a dough with the milk, then roll out on a floured board to about 20cm (8in) square and approximately 5mm (¼in) thick.

Peel, core and chop the apples, then spread on the pastry. Sprinkle with the sugar and spice and roll up like a Swiss roll. Cut into 2.5cm (1in) slices and arrange in a buttered 1.2 litre (2 pint) ovenproof dish.

Strain the lemon rind from the prepared syrup and pour over the pudding. Bake for about 30 minutes, or until puffed up and golden. Serve hot with Vanilla Custard Sauce (see page 35) or clotted cream.

NOTTINGHAM PUDDING

Also known as Apple-In-and-Out, this pudding is a combination of apple and batter, dating back to medieval days when dried fruits, spices and candied peel were put in a batter pudding and served with joints of meat. This tradition has continued in the north of England, where any leftovers are served after the meal with melted butter and treacle, lemon juice and sugar or warmed honey and cinnamon.

115g (4oz) plain flour
Pinch of salt
1 large egg
150ml (¼ pint) full-cream milk
150ml (¼ pint) water
450g (1lb) cooking apples
40g (1½oz) butter
Grated rind of ½ lemon
½ teaspoon ground cinnamon
70g (2½oz) soft brown sugar
40g (1½oz) margarine

Serves 4–6

Sieve the flour and salt together into a basin and make a well in the centre. Break the egg into the well and stir to mix with the flour. Gradually add half the milk and water, beating well with a wooden spoon until the batter is smooth and creamy. Add the remaining liquid, beating with a rotary or electric whisk to keep the batter smooth and light. Leave to stand in a cool place for about 30 minutes.

Peel, core and slice the apples. Melt the butter in a heavy frying pan, add the apples, lemon rind, cinnamon and sugar, cover and cook gently until the apples are just tender.

Put the margarine in a 19cm (7½in) square baking tin and heat near the top of a preheated oven at 220°C, 425°F, gas mark 7 until the fat is smoking. Remove from the oven, carefully add the apple mixture and pour over the batter. Return to the oven for about 20 minutes, then reduce the temperature to 190°C, 375°F, gas mark 5 for a further 20–25 minutes or until the batter is firm and golden brown (this batter pudding will not rise as much as a Yorkshire pudding because of the fruit it contains).

APPLE COBS

Also known as Bombard'd Apples or Apple Dumplings. The original dumplings were boiled, but in this recipe they are baked. Use a really good-quality cooking apple, which will go soft and puffy when cooked. You can use shortcrust or puff pastry, instead of suet-crust pastry if you want a less rich pudding.

350g (12oz) self-raising flour
Pinch of salt
175g (6oz) suet
50g (1¾oz) caster sugar
About 150ml (¼ pint)
    ice-cold water
6 medium Bramley apples
2 tablespoons mincemeat
6 cloves
Water or milk for brushing
1 egg white, beaten
3 tablespoons clotted cream
    (optional)

Serves 6

Sieve the flour and salt together into a mixing bowl. Mix in the suet and stir in half the sugar. Add just sufficient water to mix to a soft but not sticky dough. Turn out on to a lightly floured board and divide into 6 equal pieces. Roll out each piece thinly into a square large enough to encase an apple. Peel and core the apples and place one in the centre of each pastry square. Fill each apple centre with mincemeat and top with a clove. Brush the edge of each pastry square with a little water or milk, draw up the corners to meet over the centre of each apple and press the edges firmly together. Turn upside down, and place on a greased baking tray. Roll out the pastry trimmings to make small leaves to decorate the dumplings, then brush all over with the egg white and sprinkle with the remaining sugar.

Bake in the centre of a preheated oven at 200°C, 400°F, gas mark 6 for 30 minutes or until golden brown. Remove from the oven and leave to stand for a few minutes on a warm serving dish. Cut a hole in the top of each dumpling and spoon in some clotted cream, or serve with Vanilla Custard Sauce (see page 35).

VARIATION
APPLE AND BLACKBERRY COBS
Fill the apples with blackberries (or other soft fruits), a little sugar and a knob of butter instead of mincemeat.

Right: Apple Cobs

CHERRY BATTER

This famous pudding from Kent has been eaten since the 13th century, but probably the idea of combining cherries with batter came to the UK with the Normans. This dish is a reminder that Kent was one of the first counties to be colonized by the invaders. A very similar dish called Clafoutis is still made in France. Kent's famous black morello cherries, said to be the best in the world, should be used to make this delicious pudding, but drained tinned black cherries can be used out of season.

50g (1¾oz) plain flour
Pinch of salt
50g (1¾oz) caster sugar
2 eggs
300ml (½ pint) single cream or
    full-cream milk
1 tablespoon cherry brandy or a
    few drops of vanilla essence
25g (1oz) melted butter
450g (1lb) ripe black cherries,
    stoned
Icing sugar for dusting
Whipped cream to serve
    (optional)

Serves 6

Sieve the flour and salt together into a bowl. Stir in the caster sugar. Beat the eggs and blend gradually into the flour mixture. Warm the cream or milk and add slowly to the flour mixture, beating vigorously to make a smooth, light batter. Stir in the cherry brandy or vanilla essence and whisk in the melted butter. Put aside to rest while you stone the cherries.

Generously butter a shallow 600ml (1 pint) ovenproof porcelain dish or a 20cm (8in) flan tin. Spread the prepared cherries over the bottom of the dish or tin and carefully pour over the batter. Dot with a few tiny pieces of butter and bake in the centre of a preheated oven at 200°C, 400°F, gas mark 6 for 20 minutes, then reduce the temperature to 190°C, 375°F, gas mark 5 and cook for a further 20 minutes or until the batter is well risen and golden, but still creamy inside. Serve warm, generously dusted with sieved icing sugar and with whipped cream or Vanilla Custard Sauce (see page 35). If you want to serve the pudding cold, remove from the dish or tin and serve with either pouring or whipped cream.

Left: Cherry Batter

GINGERBREAD AND PEAR UPSIDE-DOWN PUDDING

This was a popular pudding in Victorian days and looks very attractive. You can bake it in either a round or a square tin.

50g (1¾oz) butter

140g (5oz) soft brown sugar

3 firm pears

6 glacé cherries

6 walnut halves

115g (4oz) margarine or lard

115g (4oz) black treacle

115g (4oz) golden syrup

225g (8oz) plain flour

¼ teaspoon salt

Pinch of ground cloves

2 teaspoons ground cinnamon

2 teaspoons ground ginger

¼ teaspoon grated nutmeg

1 level teaspoon bicarbonate
    of soda

150ml (¼ pint) warm
    full-cream milk

2 eggs

Serves 6

Line the bottom and sides of a 20cm (8in) round cake tin with buttered greaseproof paper. Melt the butter in a saucepan over a gentle heat, add 70g (2½oz) brown sugar and stir for a few minutes until dissolved. Pour into the bottom of the tin. Peel, halve and core the pears and put a glacé cherry in the centre of each pear half. Arrange the pears in a circle cut-side down on the butter-and-sugar mixture with their stalk ends facing the centre of the tin. Place the walnut halves, cut-side down, between the pears.

Put the margarine or lard, black treacle, golden syrup and the remaining brown sugar in a saucepan and melt over a low heat. Sieve the flour, salt and spices together into a mixing bowl. Dissolve the soda in warm milk. Beat the eggs and add to the milk mixture when it has cooled a little. Make a well in the centre of the dry ingredients and pour in the melted treacle mixture, followed by the egg mixture. Stir together and beat thoroughly until a smooth batter is formed. Pour carefully over the pears and walnuts. Bake in the centre of a preheated oven at 180°C, 350°F, gas mark 4 for 40–50 minutes or until well risen and firm (test with a skewer; it should come out clean). Remove from the oven and allow to shrink a little before turning out on to a warmed serving plate. Take great care when peeling off the greaseproof paper.

Serve warm with cream or Vanilla Custard Sauce (see page 35).

DAMSON COBBLER

This pudding presumably takes its name from the scone topping, which does look rather like cobblestones. You can either cut out the dough into circles and place them round the edges of the dish, overlapping each other, or you can lay the dough over like a pie crust and cut it into squares – either way, it is a delicious and economical pudding. Many fruits can be used instead of damsons – plums, greengages, blackcurrants, blackberries, apples, rhubarb, bilberries and gooseberries.

900g (2lb) damsons
250g (9oz) caster sugar
150ml (¼ pint) water
225g (8oz) self-raising flour
Pinch of salt
55g (2oz) butter
1 egg
1–2 tablespoons milk
Granulated sugar for sprinkling

Serves 6

Wash the damsons and cook slowly in a heavy saucepan with 225g (8oz) sugar and the water until just tender. Remove the stones and turn into a buttered ovenproof dish. Leave to cool.

Sieve the flour and salt together into a mixing bowl. Stir in the remaining sugar and rub in the butter. Beat the egg and add to the mixture with enough milk to make a soft dough. Roll out on a lightly floured board to about 1cm (½in) thick. Cut out the dough into rounds with a 5cm (2in) cutter and arrange in a ring around the edge of the dish of fruit with the rounds overlapping each other. Brush the scone topping with a little milk, and bake near the top of a preheated oven at 220°C, 425°F, gas mark 7 for 10 minutes. Reduce the oven temperature to 190°C, 375°F, gas mark 5. Sprinkle the top generously with granulated sugar and bake for a further 5–10 minutes until well risen and golden brown.

TEWKESBURY SAUCER BATTERS

Saucers were used for baking small savoury and sweet pies and puddings years before they were used under teacups, and a few recipes still survive. This one comes from Gloucestershire and is for batter puddings baked in saucers. You can serve them filled with fresh soft fruit such as raspberries, blackberries, loganberries or strawberries. They make a very unusual pudding for a dinner party. The quantities given here will make 4 saucer batters, which will be enough for 8 people.

225g (8oz) plain flour
¼ teaspoon salt
2 eggs, separated
600ml (1 pint) milk
700g (1lb 9oz) soft fruit
115–175g (4–6oz) caster sugar

Serves 4–8

Sieve the flour and salt together into a mixing bowl. Make a well in the centre and put in the egg yolks. Beat in the egg yolks gradually, adding the milk a little at a time and beating continuously until the mixture becomes a smooth, creamy batter. Leave in a cool place for at least 30 minutes, for the starch to begin to break down.

Meanwhile, well butter 4 ovenproof saucers. Put the fruit in an ovenproof dish and sprinkle with sugar, cover and put in the oven while it is heating up until the juices begin to run. Taste to see if it is sweet enough (be careful not to cook strawberries for more than a few seconds or they will go mushy). Take the fruit from the oven and leave on one side.

Whisk the egg whites until very stiff and fold into the batter. Divide the batter between the 4 prepared saucers, and put in the top of a preheated oven at 230°C, 450°F, gas mark 8. Bake for about 15–20 minutes or until golden brown and coming away from the edges of the saucers. Remove from the oven when cooked, and slide on to a warmed serving dish. Sprinkle with caster sugar and fill each batter with fruit. Serve hot, with whipped cream.

PLUM AND CINNAMON CRUMBLE

Crumbles can be varied not just by using seasonal fruit but also by changing the crumble topping, adding porridge oats (as here), dessicated coconut, chopped nuts, different spices and so on. Classic combinations such as rhubarb and ginger, apple and cinnamon or gooseberry and elderflower can always be relied on. This recipe was given to me by the chef at Cotehele, a medieval house belonging to the National Trust on the banks of the River Tamar in Cornwall. He cooks the crumble in individual dishes under the grill.

600g (1 lb 5oz) English plums,
    stoned
50g (1¾oz) light brown sugar
½ teaspoon ground cinnamon

FOR THE TOPPING
40g (1½oz) butter, cut into
    small pieces
55g (2oz) plain flour
½ teaspoon cinnamon
40g (1½oz) light brown sugar
60g (2oz) porridge oats

Serves 4

Poach the plums with the sugar and cinnamon and a very little water until just tender. Remove from the heat and tip into a buttered ovenproof baking dish. Rub the butter into the flour and cinnamon, sieved together into a mixing bowl, until the mixture resembles breadcrumbs. Stir in the sugar and oats. Sprinkle evenly over the plums and bake in a preheated oven at 180°C, 350°F, gas mark 4 for about 25 minutes, or until golden brown. Remove from the oven and leave to cool a little. Eat warm and serve with Vanilla Custard Sauce (see page 35), ice cream or clotted cream.

RHUBARB AND ORANGE BETTY

An original 19th-century Brown Betty was made with apples, breadcrumbs and suet and was a popular pudding with lower-paid countryfolk. Delicious Brown Betty can be made with other fruits, but the amount of sugar must be adjusted accordingly. Some of the most successful are rhubarb (as here), plums, gooseberries, damsons, blackcurrants, blackberries and cherries.

85g (3oz) butter
115g (4oz) fresh white
   breadcrumbs
450g (1lb) rhubarb
85–115g (3–4 oz) caster or
   soft brown sugar
Grated rind and juice of
   1 orange

Serves 4–6

Melt the butter in a heavy frying pan, add the breadcrumbs and cook over a moderate heat, stirring continuously to prevent burning, until the crumbs are light golden in colour.

Cut the rhubarb into 2.5cm (1in) lengths, then mix with the sugar, orange rind and juice. Butter a 1.2 litre (2 pint) ovenproof dish and fill with alternate layers of rhubarb and breadcrumbs, finishing with a layer of crumbs. Sprinkle with extra sugar and cover with foil. Bake in the centre of a preheated oven at 180°C, 350°F, gas mark 4 for 20 minutes, then remove the foil and continue cooking for a further 25–30 minutes, or until the top is brown and crisp and the rhubarb underneath is soft.

Serve hot with Vanilla Custard Sauce (see page 35) or cream.

THE CURATE'S PUDDING

This recipe comes from The Best of Eliza Acton, *first published in 1845. It's an excellent pudding best made with seasonal British fruits. I use thinly sliced brioche buns instead of 'penny rolls', but bread rolls or slices of bread work just as well.*

450g (1lb) young pink rhubarb
25g (1oz) butter
4 tablespoons caster sugar
2 brioche buns, thinly sliced

Serves 4

Cut the rhubarb into 2.5cm (1in) lengths. Melt the butter and brush the insides of a 1.2 litre (2 pint) soufflé dish or ovenproof dish with a little of it. Place half the rhubarb into the dish and sprinkle on about half the sugar. Cover the fruit with a layer of brioche slices, reserving enough for a second layer of brioche slices.

Now lay on the remaining fruit and sprinkle on all but a teaspoon of the remaining sugar. Cover the rhubarb with slices of brioche, shaping to fit. Press down with your hand to flatten the pudding, then brush the top with the remaining butter. Sprinkle with the remaining sugar and bake in a preheated oven at 180°C, 350°F, gas mark 4 for about 30 minutes, or until the fruit is tender and the top browned. Serve warm with cream.

FIGS BAKED IN WINE

In the past, figs have been much more popular in British cookery than they are now. They were ripened in sheltered gardens in the south of England. There is something rather luxurious about fresh figs for pudding.

40g (1½oz) butter, at room
    temperature
12 fresh ripe figs
1½ teaspoons vanilla extract
115g (4oz) demerara sugar,
    or 4 tablespoons clear honey
100ml (3½fl oz) white wine
50ml (2fl oz) Marsala

Serves 4–6

Preheat the oven to 180°C, 350°F, gas mark 4. Smear the butter on a shallow ovenproof dish, large enough to hold all the figs snugly together. Wash and dry the figs, then cut a deep cross in their tops, without cutting through them completely. Arrange them in the dish, sprinkle with vanilla extract and sugar or honey, then pour the wine and Marsala around the figs.

Cover with foil and put on a high shelf in the oven for 20 minutes, then uncover and cook for a further 20 minutes.

Serve 2 figs per person with thick cream or ice cream and the syrup drizzled around the dish.

VARIATION
FIGS BAKED IN CLARET
Bake figs in claret instead of white wine and substitute 2 tablespoons sugar for the 115g (4oz) sugar or the honey.

JAM ROLY-POLY

This popular pudding used to be boiled in a cloth or shirtsleeve, but baking gives the pastry a lovely crisp crust, which is usually more popular with children. Mincemeat or golden syrup can be used instead of jam. Traditionally this was a suet roly-poly pudding with meat at one end and fruit or jam at the other. It was originally devised for the straw-hat makers of Luton to provide a complete meal while they were away at work, as was the Cornish pasty for the tin miners of Cornwall.

225g (8oz) self-raising flour
1 teaspoon mixed spice
   (optional)
Pinch of salt
115g (4oz) suet
About 8 tablespoons water
4–5 tablespoons good-quality
   jam, warmed
Milk, for brushing
1 egg, beaten, to glaze
Caster sugar for sprinkling

Serves 4–6

Sieve the flour, spice (if using) and salt together into a mixing bowl. Stir in the suet and add just enough water to mix to a soft, but not sticky, dough. Turn out on to a lightly floured board and roll into a rectangle about 20 x 30cm (8 x 12in). Spread evenly with warm jam, leaving a 1cm (½in) border all the way around. Fold this border over the jam and brush with milk. Roll up fairly loosely and press the edges of the dough together to seal them. Put in a lightly buttered roasting tin and brush with beaten egg. Sprinkle with caster sugar.

Bake in the centre of a preheated oven at 200°C, 400°F, gas mark 6, with the tin propped up so that the roly-poly rolls into one end, which helps to keep its shape. Cook for 35–40 minutes or until golden brown.

Serve warm, sprinkled with extra caster sugar and Vanilla Custard Sauce (see page 35).

VARIATION
BEDFORDSHIRE CLANGER
Cook 450g (1lb) peeled, cored and thinly sliced cooking apples briefly with a little butter and 85g (3oz) caster sugar until tender. Leave to cool, then spread over the pastry, roll up and cook as before.

BREAD-AND-BUTTER PUDDING

Bread-and-butter pudding was in the recipe books by the 1720s, when it was made of freshly sliced and buttered bread with currants, beaten eggs and nutmeg. It was only in Victorian times that it became a means of putting stale bread to good use. Since then it has become a British institution and there are dozens of versions. Modern recipes sometimes add fresh or poached fruit, marmalade, apricot jam or chocolate and use brioche, fruit loaf, panettone and croissants.

300ml (½ pint) full-cream or Jersey milk

300ml (½ pint) double cream

1 vanilla pod, split in half lengthways

4–6 slices cut from a good-quality white sandwich loaf

About 100g (3½oz) butter, softened

55g (2oz) sultanas, soaked in hot water until plump

25g (1oz) candied peel, chopped (optional)

3 large eggs

About 70g (2½oz) caster sugar

Freshly grated nutmeg

Icing sugar for dusting

Serves 6

Slowly heat the milk and cream with the vanilla pod, including its scraped-out seeds, until boiling point is just reached. Take off the heat and leave to cool a little.

Remove the crusts from the bread and butter generously. Cut each slice into 4 triangles, then arrange, overlapping in the base of a well-buttered 1.5 litre (2¾ pint) ovenproof dish. Sprinkle with the soaked and drained sultanas and candied peel, if using.

Whisk the eggs with the sugar, then pour into a jug with the strained milk and cream mixture. Taste and add more sugar, if you wish. Whisk again, then carefully pour evenly over the bread, making sure that each triangle gets a good soaking (add more milk if the liquid doesn't cover the bread). Grate plenty of nutmeg over the surface, cover and leave to soak for at least 2 hours, preferably overnight, in the refrigerator. When ready to cook, place the dish in a roasting tin filled with hot water to the level of the top of the custard.

Bake in a preheated oven at 150°C, 300°F, gas mark 2 for 1–1¼ hours until just set and golden (after 30 minutes cooking time, dust with icing sugar to crisp up the top). Rest for 20 minutes before serving. No extra cream is really necessary as the custard is very rich and delicious.

OLD-FASHIONED BREAD PUD

In Plymouth, this very old pudding is called Nelson's Cake after the great man who was obviously a lover of it. It is also particularly popular in East Anglia, where Nelson was born. The original version would have been boiled but it is now more commonly baked. Individual bread puddings were fashionable in Georgian times – they were baked in buttered teacups.

225g (8oz) stale white or brown
    bread, with crusts removed
300ml (½ pint) milk
2 tablespoons brandy (optional)
50g (1¾oz) melted butter
    or suet
50g (1¾oz) soft brown sugar
2 level teaspoons mixed spice
1 egg, beaten
175g (6oz) mixed dried fruit
Grated rind of 1 lemon
Grated rind of ½ orange
Freshly grated nutmeg
Caster sugar for sprinkling

Serves 4

Break the bread into small pieces and put in a large mixing bowl. Pour over the milk and brandy, if using, stir well and leave to soak for at least 30 minutes.

Add the melted butter or suet, sugar, spice and egg then, using a fork, beat out any lumps. Stir in the dried fruit and grated lemon and orange rind, then turn the mixture into a buttered 1.2 litre (2 pint) ovenproof dish. Grate nutmeg over the top.

Bake in a preheated oven at 180°C, 350°F, gas mark 4 for 1¼–1½ hours until nicely brown on top.

Serve hot, sprinkled with caster sugar and with Vanilla Custard Sauce (see page 35) or a hard sauce such as Brandy and Lemon butter (see page 55).

VARIATION
OLD-FASHIONED ICED BREAD PUD
Make as before, but remove from the oven after 1 hour. Cover with meringue made from 2 egg whites and 115g (4oz) caster sugar. Put back in the oven and cook for a further 20 minutes, or until the meringue is crisp and lightly browned.

SPICY GROUND RICE PUDDING

This recipe is based on one by Eliza Acton, one of the best known of the 19th-century cookery writers. Eggs are added to make a richer pudding. Pies and puddings were often 'iced' or topped with egg whites as in this recipe.

40g (1½oz) ground rice
   or semolina
600ml (1 pint) full-cream milk
Strip of lemon peel
1 vanilla pod
1 bay leaf
Pinch of ground nutmeg
25g (1oz) caster sugar or
   ½ tablespoon honey
2 eggs, separated
25g (1oz) butter
Grated nutmeg or ground
   cinnamon for sprinkling
115g (4oz) caster sugar

Serves 4–6

Butter thoroughly a 1.2 litre (2 pint) ovenproof dish. Mix the ground rice or semolina to a smooth paste with a little of the milk in a basin. Boil the rest of the milk with the lemon peel, vanilla pod, bay leaf and pinch of nutmeg. Pour on to the ground rice or semolina, stirring continuously. Rinse the pan in which the milk was boiled and leave a film of cold water on the bottom. Return the rice and milk to the pan and bring slowly to the boil again, stirring all the time so that it does not burn on the bottom. Cook gently for 10 minutes. Add the sugar or honey. Beat the egg yolks and beat into the rice. Remove the vanilla pod, bay leaf and lemon peel. Pour into the prepared pie dish. Dot with butter and sprinkle with nutmeg or cinnamon. Bake in the centre of a preheated oven at 180°C, 350°F, gas mark 4 for about 25 minutes. Whisk the egg whites until stiff and whisk in 50g (1¾oz) caster sugar.

Fold in the remaining caster sugar. Pile the sweetened egg whites on top of the pudding and bake for a further 20 minutes, until the meringue is crisp and lightly browned. Serve hot with pouring cream and a fruit sauce.

VARIATION
Try edging the pie dish with puff pastry, or adding 50g (2oz) currants, sultanas or raisins and 25g (1oz) candied peel.

CHOCOLATE PUDDLE PUDDING

A firm family favourite, this pudding emerges from the oven with its own built-in sauce hidden under a layer of chocolate sponge. Its exact origin is vague, although it has been around for years.

FOR THE PUDDING
115g (4oz) butter, softened
115g (4oz) soft light brown
    sugar
1 teaspoon vanilla extract
2 large eggs, beaten
85g (3oz) self-raising flour
25g (1oz) cocoa powder
A little milk

FOR THE SAUCE
85g (3oz) light brown sugar
25g (1oz) cocoa powder
300ml (½ pint) full-cream milk

Serves 4–6

Preheat the oven to 180°C, 350°F, gas mark 4. Cream the butter and sugar together until light and fluffy. Beat in the vanilla extract, then gradually beat in the eggs.

Sieve the flour and cocoa together, then fold into the creamed mixture. Mix in just enough milk to give a soft dropping consistency. Spoon into a buttered 1.2 litre (2 pint) ovenproof dish.

For the sauce, mix the sugar and cocoa together and gradually beat in the milk. Pour evenly over the pudding mixture and bake for 40–60 minutes, or until just set in the centre. (If the pudding is a bit too soft in the centre, the sauce will be thin when you cut into the pudding, but if you overcook so that the pudding is very firm in the centre, the sauce will disappear. The centre should spring back when you press it lightly with your fingertips.) Leave to stand for 5 minutes. Serve with cream.

ICKY STICKY TOFFEE SPONGE

A top favourite with most people, the original recipe for this pudding probably dates back to the 1930s. It was made famous in the 1960s by the late, great Francis Coulson, chef and proprietor of the Sharrow Bay Country House Hotel in Ullswater, Cumbria.

FOR THE SPONGE
50g (1¾oz) butter
175g (6oz) granulated sugar
175g (6oz) dates, stoned and
    chopped
300ml (½ pint) water
1 teaspoon bicarbonate of soda
2 large eggs
175g (6oz) self-raising flour
A few drops of vanilla extract

FOR THE SAUCE
40g (1½oz) demerara sugar
1 tablespoon black treacle,
    golden syrup or honey
300ml (½ pint) double cream

Serves 6–8

To make the sponge, cream the butter and sugar together. Boil the chopped dates in the water for about 10 minutes or until soft, then add the bicarbonate of soda. Beat the eggs into the creamed mixture, followed by the sieved flour, dates with their liquid and vanilla extract. Pour into a buttered 20cm (8in) round, loose-bottomed cake tin that is at least 7.5cm (3in) deep. Bake in a preheated oven at 180°C, 350°F, gas mark 4 for about 40 minutes, or until firm to the touch.

Meanwhile, make the toffee sauce. Put the sugar and treacle in a pan and heat gently, stirring until the sugar has dissolved. Stir in the cream and bring to the boil. Remove from the heat and leave to stand until needed.

When the pudding is cooked, remove from the oven and leave for 5 minutes, then turn out on to a warm serving plate. Pour over the sauce. Put under the grill for a few minutes until the sauce bubbles, then serve with ice cream.

PEARS IN NIGHTSHIRTS

The combination of apples and pears is a very old one, as they were the first two fruits to be grown in Britain. For this recipe, the pears are poached in cider, set on a bed of apple pulp and coated with a layer of crisp, pale brown meringue – 'the nightshirts'.

6 large firm dessert pears
425ml (¾ pint) cider
700g (1lb 9oz) cooking apples
15g (½oz) butter
Grated rind of 1 lemon
1 tablespoon lemon juice
2–3 cloves
85g–115g (3–4oz) caster sugar
85g (3oz) icing sugar, sifted
6 egg whites
350g (12oz) caster sugar
50g (1¾oz) toasted flaked
   almonds

Serves 6

Peel the pears, but leave on the stalks. Put the cider into a saucepan large enough to take the pears. Bring to the boil and lower the pears gently into this liquor. Cover and simmer very gently for 30–35 minutes or until the pears are translucent and just tender.

While the pears are cooking, make the apple pulp. Peel, core and slice the apples. Rub the butter over the sides and bottom of a saucepan. Add the apple slices, lemon rind, lemon juice and cloves. Cover with buttered greaseproof paper and cook over a low heat for about 15 minutes, until the apples are soft and any liquid has evaporated. Stir gently from time to time. Remove the cloves and beat the apples to a smooth, thick pulp with a wooden spoon. Add sugar to taste. Pour into a buttered ovenproof dish large enough to take the pears, allowing room for the meringue coating.

Drain the cooked pears and roll each one in sifted icing sugar. Place the pears on top of the apple pulp. Whisk the egg whites until very stiff. Add 175g (6oz) caster sugar and whisk until stiff and glossy. Fold in the remaining 175g (6oz) caster sugar and spread or pipe a thick coating of meringue over the pears. Bake in a preheated oven at 200°C, 400°F, gas mark 6 for 10–15 minutes or until the meringue is crisp and light brown. Serve immediately, sprinkled with toasted flaked almonds.

HOLLYGOG PUDDING

This is a golden-syrupy roly-poly which is baked in milk. It was first made in the Oxfordshire village of Kiddington, where it has been passed down among farming families.

225g (8oz) plain flour
Pinch of salt
115g (4oz) butter
About 3 tablespoons cold water
4 tablespoons golden syrup,
    warmed
About 300ml (½ pint)
    full-cream milk

FOR THE CUSTARD SAUCE
300ml (½ pint) full-cream milk
150ml (¼ pint) single cream
1 vanilla pod or strip of
    lemon peel
3 eggs
2 level tablespoons caster sugar
2 heaped tablespoons cornflour
4 tablespoons milk

Serves 4–6

Right: Hollygog Pudding
Next page: Pears in Nightshirts

Sieve the flour and salt into a mixing bowl and rub in the butter until the mixture resembles breadcrumbs. Add water to form a stiff dough. Roll out into a rectangular strip, spread with syrup and roll up like a Swiss roll. Put in a well-buttered oval ovenproof dish and pour over enough milk to come halfway up the side of the pudding. Bake in a preheated oven at 200°C, 400°F, gas mark 6 for 40–45 minutes. Serve hot in slices with cream, Economical Custard Sauce (see below) or Vanilla Custard Sauce (see page 35).

ECONOMICAL CUSTARD SAUCE

Heat the milk and cream in a saucepan (you can use all milk if you prefer) with the vanilla pod or lemon peel. Bring to the boil. Remove from the heat and leave to cool for a few seconds, removing the vanilla pod or lemon peel. Beat the eggs with sugar in a basin. Mix the cornflour with 4 tablespoons milk to make a smooth paste. Add this to the egg mixture and stir well. Pour the hot milk slowly on to the egg mixture, stirring continuously. Rinse out the saucepan, leaving a film of cold water in the bottom. Return the custard to the pan and stir with a wooden spoon over a low heat until thick (don't boil the custard or it will curdle). Strain into a jug and serve hot. If you don't want a skin to form on top of your custard, sprinkle the surface with caster sugar or cover closely with a piece of damp greaseproof paper or clingfilm.

QUEEN'S PUDDING

Also called Queen of Puddings, this dish was named after Queen Victoria and created by her chefs at Buckingham Palace, but it was, in fact, based on a much older 17th-century recipe – a milk pudding thickened with breadcrumbs and eggs. It was originally baked in a 'puff paste' case. Try using lemon or lime curd instead of jam.

85g (3oz) fresh white
    breadcrumbs
3 eggs, separated
200g (7oz) caster sugar
600ml (1 pint) full-cream milk
25g (1oz) butter
Grated rind of ½ lemon
3 tablespoons raspberry jam

Serves 6

Butter a 1.2 litre (2 pint) ovenproof dish. Sprinkle the breadcrumbs in the bottom of the dish. Beat the egg yolks with 25g (1oz) caster sugar. Put the milk, butter and grated lemon rind into a saucepan and bring slowly to the boil. Leave to cool a little and then pour on to the yolks, stirring continuously until the mixture is smooth. Strain the custard over the breadcrumbs and leave to soak for at least 15 minutes. Stand the dish in a roasting tin half-filled with hot water and bake in the centre of a preheated oven at 180°C, 350°F, gas mark 4 for 25–30 minutes, or until lightly set. Warm the jam and spread over the top of the pudding. Whisk the egg whites until very stiff and add 85g (3oz) caster sugar. Whisk again until stiff and glossy. Fold in the remaining sugar. Pile or pipe the meringue on top of the jam. Sprinkle with extra sugar and bake for a further 15–20 minutes, or until the meringue is crisp and lightly browned.

Serve warm, with or without Jam Sauce (see page 67) and pouring cream, or cold with fresh raspberries and cream.

VARIATION
MANCHESTER PUDDING
Put a layer of apricot jam in the bottom of an ovenproof dish. Continue as before, but include 2 tablespoons of sherry or brandy in the custard. When the pudding is lightly set, spread with more apricot jam, and top with meringue as before.

Left: Queen's Pudding
Previous page: Baked Quinces in Cinnamon Syrup

BAKED QUINCES IN CINNAMON SYRUP

Quinces have been grown in Britain since Anglo-Saxon times, when they were probably eaten stewed with honey. The first marmalade to arrive here in medieval days from southern Europe was made from the fruit (marmelo is Portuguese for 'quince') and in Elizabethan times the fruit was particularly highly regarded. So we have had a long love affair with the quince – and hurray, it is back in fashion. If you have room in your garden, plant an old-fashioned quince tree – it is a thing of beauty all year round.

6 quinces
Juice of 2 lemons
200g (7oz) caster sugar
1 vanilla pod, split in half
    lengthways
About 300ml (½ pint) water
1 small stick of cinnamon
4 cloves

Serves 4

Peel 4 of the quinces and cut into quarters. Remove the cores and place in a large heavy-lidded ovenproof dish, arranging the fruit in a single layer. Pour over the lemon juice to prevent discolouration.

Use the remaining 2 quinces to make the syrup. Peel, core and chop them coarsely, then place in a pan with half the sugar and the vanilla-pod seeds. Add enough water to cover. Bring to the boil and simmer for about 1 hour, or until the quinces are very soft and the liquid has turned syrupy. Strain and discard the quince pulp.

Pour the syrup over the prepared quince quarters, adding the cinnamon, cloves and remaining sugar. Make sure the quinces are covered by the syrup, adding a little more water if necessary. Place a piece of greaseproof paper on top to keep the fruit submerged.

Cover with the lid of the pan and place in a preheated oven at 130°C, 250°F, gas mark ½ and cook for 2–3 hours, or until the quinces are soft to touch and golden in colour.

Serve warm with either Vanilla Custard Sauce (see opposite), ice cream or thick cream.

VANILLA CUSTARD SAUCE

This classic custard sauce goes beautifully with almost all the dishes in this book.

6 large egg yolks
70g (2½oz) caster sugar
1 vanilla pod
300ml (½ pint) full-cream milk
300ml (½ pint) double cream

Beat the egg yolks and sugar together in a bowl until well blended. Split and scrape the seeds of the vanilla pod into a pan with the milk and cream and bring to the boil. Place the bowl over a pan of hot water and whisk the cream into the egg mixture. As the egg yolks warm, the cream will thicken to create a custard. Keep stirring until it coats the back of a spoon. Remove the bowl from the heat and serve warm or cold.

VARIATIONS

GINGER CUSTARD
Add 75g (3oz) finely chopped stem ginger to the milk and cream instead of the vanilla pod.

LEMON (ORANGE) CUSTARD
Add the grated rind of 2 lemons or 2 oranges to the milk and cream instead of the vanilla pod.

PIES, TARTS AND FLANS

The British have as great a claim as any nation to being experts in the art of pie- and tart-making. Their recipes for sweet pies and tarts have hardly changed over the centuries since the Middle Ages. The majority of the populace had to take their pies to communal ovens or pie-makers to be baked as the equipment, space, fuel and technology were only available to the relatively well-off.

The pie developed from the Roman idea of sealing meat or fish inside a flour and oil paste to cook it. This paste case or 'coffyn' was not eaten, but discarded or given to the dogs. By medieval times in northern Europe, where butter and lard were the common cooking fats, pastry began to be made that was strong and pliable enough to be moulded into a free-standing container. Thus the 'stand' pie was invented – the ancestor of our modern 'raised' pie.

By the 15th century, pies had become very popular and there was an enormous variety. Most meat and fish pies included dried fruit, spices, apples, gooseberries, sugar and honey so it was not easy to tell a savoury from a sweet pie. By Elizabethan times, shorter, richer pastry was being made, sometimes including butter and eggs. Pies became more and more elaborate.

Sweetened meat and dried fruit pies and standing pies began to go out of fashion in the Georgian period. Fruit tarts and pies were becoming much more adventurous and were now prepared in dishes or tins – the 'dish pye'. A large variety of fruits were put into pies, together with luxurious fillings like chocolate, chestnuts and almonds. Many of these recipes have remained more or less in their original form.

Tarts were made of short rich pastry, which became richer and shorter as the centuries progressed. Really rich bitter paste or 'puff paste' was used in Elizabethan times to make fruit tarts and, later, for jam tarts and patties. Some Elizabethan tart fillings or 'tartstuff' might seem strange to modern tastes – prunes, medlars, quinces and rosehips were stewed with sugar, red wine, cinnamon, ginger and rose-water. Flowers prepared in the spring and summer were also popular as tart fillings.

There is such an enormous variety of pies, tarts and flans, all interesting historically and good to eat, that I have found it extremely difficult to choose just a few for this book. I have tried to include some of the old favourites as well as others that might have been long forgotten.

APPLE AND CHEESECRUST PIE

British apples are among the best in the world. Even the most chauvinistic of the world's 'grandes cuisines' are compelled to acknowledge their quality, as well as that of English apple pie, which is at its traditional best served with cream, or good English Cheddar or Wensleydale cheese, and must surely rank among the world's top puddings. The traditional combination of apple and cheese has inspired the use of cheese pastry in this recipe.

FOR THE CHEESE PASTRY
175g (6oz) plain flour
115g (4oz) butter, cut in
   small pieces
115g (4oz) Cheddar cheese,
   finely grated
1 egg yolk
About 1 tablespoon
   ice-cold water

FOR THE FILLING
700g (1lb 9oz) Bramley apples
225g (8oz) Cox's apples
50g (1¾oz) butter
85g (3oz) soft brown sugar
Pinch of ground cinnamon
Grated rind of ½ lemon
50g (1¾oz) raisins (optional)
Juice of 1 lemon
A little milk and caster sugar

Serves 6

To make the cheese pastry, sieve the flour into a mixing bowl, then rub in the butter. Stir in the grated cheese, then mix to a dough with the egg yolk and water. Knead lightly, then chill in the refrigerator.

Cut each apple into thick slices and fry gently in the butter, sprinkling with sugar. Add the cinnamon and lemon rind, then place in a shallow, buttered 23cm (9in) pie dish with the raisins, if using. Pour over the lemon juice and leave to cool.

Roll out the chilled pastry and use to make a lid for the pie. Decorate as you wish, make a hole in the centre, then brush with milk and sprinkle with caster sugar. Bake in a preheated oven at 190°C, 375°F, gas mark 5 for 20–30 minutes, or until the apples are tender and the pastry is golden brown.

Serve warm with Vanilla Custard Sauce (see page 35) or cream.

APPLE PASTIES

A pasty refers to any sweet and savoury ingredients folded and enclosed in pastry. It is the pride of the West Country, especially Cornwall. Originally the pasty was invented for the men to take to work to keep them going through the long working day. This recipe is a very popular pudding at one of my local pubs. Any flavourings and spices can be added, and try using different combinations of fruit – apple and blackberry, apple and raspberry or apricot and gooseberry.

350g (12oz) shortcrust pastry
  (see page 10)
3–4 cooking apples
About 115g (4oz) caster or
  brown sugar
½ level teaspoon ground
  cinnamon
1 level tablespoon cornflour
2 teaspoons lemon juice
50g (1¾oz) sultanas or raisins
1 small egg
1 tablespoon cold water
Sifted icing sugar for dusting

Serves 4–6

Peel, core and slice the apples and put in a saucepan with the sugar and cinnamon. Combine the cornflour and lemon juice to make a paste and then add to the saucepan. Cook over a low heat until the apples are tender but not broken up, stirring frequently. Remove from the heat and allow to cool. Add the sultanas or raisins and taste for sweetness.

Roll out the pastry on a lightly floured board to about 3mm (⅛in) thickness and cut into 4 circles 20cm (8in) in diameter or 6 smaller circles. Divide the apple mixture between the circles, and draw up the edges of the pastry to make a seam across the top, pinching the edges together firmly. Crimp the edges together to make a neat ridge. Place on a greased baking tray and chill again.

Beat the egg with 1 tablespoon water. Brush the glaze over the pasties and make a slit in the top of each one. Bake the pasties in a preheated oven at 220°C, 425°F, gas mark 7 for 20–30 minutes or until golden brown.

Serve hot or cold with clotted or whipped cream. Try removing a small piece of pastry from the top of each pasty and putting in a dollop of clotted cream – delicious!

TAFFETY TART

These apple and orange tarts used to be a great favourite in the 18th century. Originally, apple purée was mixed with marmalade and candied orange peel, but here grated apple is combined with orange segments and baked in an orange-flavoured pastry case.

FOR THE PASTRY
175g (6oz) plain flour
50g (1¾oz) semolina
2 tablespoons icing sugar
Pinch of salt
Grated rind and juice of
   1 orange
115g (4oz) butter

FOR THE FILLING
1 large orange
2 large eggs
115g (4oz) caster sugar
1 large Bramley apple,
   peeled and grated

Serves 4–6

To make the pastry, sieve the flour, semolina, icing sugar and salt together into a mixing bowl.

Gently heat the orange rind, juice and butter in a small pan until bubbling. Remove from the heat and leave to cool for a few minutes. Gradually stir into the flour mixture to make a dough. Roll out and use to line a buttered 20cm (8in) flan tin. Prick all over and chill for about 30 minutes. Line with baking paper and baking beans. Place in the oven on the hot baking sheet and bake blind for about 10 minutes, then remove the baking parchment and beans and cook for another 10 minutes to dry out the inside without browning the pastry. Remove from the oven and cool briefly.

To make the filling, grate the rind of the orange, then remove the segments, taking off the pith and reserving as much juice as possible. Beat the eggs and sugar together well and add the orange segments, rind, juice and grated apple. Pour into the cooled pastry case and bake in a preheated oven at 180°C, 350°F, gas mark 4 for about 30 minutes until the top is golden.

Serve warm with Vanilla Custard or Creamy Marmalade Sauce (see page 35 and opposite), ice cream or cream. Also very good cold with cream.

CREAMY MARMALADE SAUCE

Try this delectable sauce with Taffety Tart or poured over vanilla ice cream.

5 rounded tablespoons good-
    quality orange marmalade
2 tablespoons apple juice
150ml (¼ pint) double cream

Put the marmalade in a small saucepan with the apple juice (if the marmalade is very coarse, chop it roughly). Melt it gently over a low heat, stirring from time to time. Pour in the cream and stir carefully until it is thoroughly mixed with the marmalade. Simmer for 3–4 minutes, until slightly thickened. Serve hot.

SEVILLE ORANGE TART

Oranges began to arrive in England at the end of the 13th century from southern Europe, but were extremely expensive and always of the bitter Seville type. It wasn't until the 16th century that sweet oranges were first brought back from Ceylon by the Portuguese.

Use Seville oranges when in season for this recipe, or sharpen sweet oranges with the juice of a lemon.

175g (6oz) sweet shortcrust
    pastry (see Raspberry and
    Cream Tart, page 44, but add
    the grated rind of ½ lemon)
Grated rind and juice of
    2 Seville oranges
60g (2oz) caster sugar
60g (2oz) cake crumbs
    (Madeira-type)
25g (1oz) butter, cut into
    small pieces
150ml (¼ pint) single cream
    or full-cream milk
2 eggs, separated

Serves 6

Roll out the pastry and use to line a 23cm (9in) flan ring. Chill, then bake blind in the usual way (see Taffety Tart, page 40). Reduce the oven to 180°C, 350°F, gas mark 4.

Mix the orange rind with the sugar until it turns yellowy-orange, then add the cake crumbs and the butter. Warm the cream or milk and pour over the mixture. Stir until the butter has melted, then stir in the egg yolks and orange juice. Whisk the egg whites until they stand in soft peaks, then fold in gently. Spoon the mixture into the pastry case and bake for 30 minutes until set and golden brown. Serve warm or cold with cream.

QUINCE AND PEAR DOUBLECRUST PIE

Quinces, pears and apples were once put into pies with wine and spices and baked for four hours. I promise you this recipe is quicker! If you have trouble buying quinces, use extra pears or apples instead.

300g (10½oz) puff pastry (see page 11)

1 egg

1 tablespoon milk

500ml (18fl oz) water

100g (3½oz) caster sugar

1 vanilla pod, split in half lengthways

3 quinces

Juice of 1 lemon

3 ripe pears

1 tablespoon redcurrant jelly

Serves 8

Bring the water, sugar and vanilla pod to the boil in a pan, then simmer gently for about 15 minutes. Peel and core the quinces and roll them in lemon juice to prevent browning. Cut into 6mm (¼in) slices and roll in the lemon juice again. Remove with a slotted spoon and poach in the vanilla sugar syrup for 45 minutes, or until the quinces turn pink and tender. Allow them to cool in this liquid. Roll the pastry out into 2 circles, 30cm (12in) in diameter and chill for 30 minutes.

Drain the quinces thoroughly in a colander or sieve and then on kitchen paper, reserving their liquor for later. Peel, core and slice the pears the same size as the quinces. Toss them in the leftover lemon juice, then mix the two fruits together well.

Lay one of the pastry discs on a buttered baking tray and pile on the fruit, leaving a border 2.5cm (1in) all around. Beat the egg with the milk and brush the border of pastry with it. Now lay the second disc of pastry over the fruit, pressing the edges together well. Using the back of a small knife, knock up the edges of the pastry and make a small hole in the top of the pie. Glaze the top with the egg mixture. Bake in a preheated oven at 200°C, 400°F, gas mark 6 for about 35 minutes, or until golden brown (be careful it doesn't burn). Reduce the reserved quince cooking liquor to about 6 tablespoons, then whisk in the redcurrant jelly.

Serve the pie lukewarm with the sauce at the same temperature.

RASPBERRY AND CREAM TART

This delicious tart recipe is based on one that dates back to the 17th century. In the original, the highly spiced raspberries were set in an egg custard and cooked in a thin-lidded puff-pastry pie. Other soft fruits like strawberries, cherries, blueberries and bilberries are successful and almond pastry (see page 47) is delicious, although more difficult to handle.

FOR THE SWEET
  SHORTCRUST PASTRY
175g (6oz) plain flour
Pinch of salt
85g (3oz) icing sugar
150g (5½oz) unsalted butter
2 small egg yolks, beaten

FOR THE FILLING
900g (2lb) fresh raspberries
About 115g (4oz) caster sugar
3 large eggs
1 level tablespoon cornflour
300ml (½ pint) single cream
1 tablespoon raspberry liqueur

Serves 6–8

To make the pastry, sieve the flour with the salt and icing sugar into a bowl. Rub in the butter, then mix to a soft dough with the egg yolks. Knead very briefly, then wrap in clingfilm and chill in the refrigerator for 30 minutes. Roll out and use to line a buttered 25cm (10in) flan tin. Chill again for 15 minutes, then bake blind in the usual way (see Taffety Tart, page 40). Remove the pastry case from the oven and leave to cool.

Reduce the oven temperature to 180°C, 350°F, gas mark 4. Fill the pastry case with raspberries and sprinkle them with 85g (3oz) caster sugar. Beat the eggs, remaining sugar and cornflour together until almost white. Stir in the cream and liqueur and taste for sweetness. Add more sugar if you wish. Pour the egg mixture over the raspberries and bake in the centre of the oven for 35–40 minutes, or until the custard has just set.

Serve warm with ice cream or cream.

A BLACKCURRANT AND CINNAMON PLATE PIE

This pie, baked on a plate, is made with cinnamon-flavoured pastry. Try experimenting with various spices and different fruits.

FOR THE PASTRY
225g (8oz) plain flour
Pinch of salt
1 dessertspoon ground
    cinnamon
50g (1¾oz) butter or margarine
50g (1¾oz) lard
3 tablespoons cold water

FOR THE FILLING
450g (1lb) fresh or frozen
    blackcurrants
115g (4oz) caster sugar
Knob of softened butter
Milk and caster sugar, for glazing

Serves 6

Sieve the flour, salt and cinnamon together into a mixing bowl. Rub in the fats until the mixture resembles breadcrumbs. Add enough water to mix to a firm dough. Knead lightly until smooth, and chill.

Put the blackcurrants and sugar in a saucepan. Cook over a gentle heat until the juices begin to run, then cook more rapidly for a few minutes, stirring frequently until the blackcurrants look thick and rich. Taste and add more sugar, if necessary. Turn into a dish and cool.

Roll out the pastry thinly on a lightly floured board. Using half the pastry, line a buttered 20–23cm (8–9in) ovenproof plate. Prick the bottom of the pastry with a fork, brush with softened butter (this will help to prevent the pastry at the bottom from going too soggy) and chill for a few minutes. Fill the plate with cooked blackcurrants. Roll out the remaining pastry to make a lid, dampening the edges and pressing together well to seal. Flute the edges of the pie. Cut a 5cm (2in) cross in the centre of the top of the pie and fold back each triangle of pastry to make an open square showing the blackcurrants. Brush the pastry with milk and sprinkle with caster sugar. Bake near the top of a preheated oven at 220°C, 425°F, gas mark 7 for 10 minutes to set the pastry and then decrease the temperature to 180°C, 350°F, gas mark 4 for a further 20–25 minutes. Serve hot or cold, sprinkled with more caster sugar and with cinnamon-flavoured whipped cream or clotted cream piled on the square of blackcurrants showing on top of the pie.

RHUBARB AND ORANGE LATTICE TART

This traditional tart is made with cinnamon- or ginger-flavoured pastry and filled with rhubarb, flavoured with orange. The lattice top is a traditional way of finishing off a pie – not for decoration but for marking. In the past, the housewife would make a large number of both savoury and sweet pies and bake them all at the same time, either in her own oven or in the village baker's oven, and of course the pies all had to be identified with either lattices, slits or marks of some description.

FOR THE PASTRY
175g (6oz) plain flour
Pinch of salt
1 teaspoon ground ginger
    or cinnamon
85g (3oz) butter
25g (1oz) caster sugar
1 egg, beaten
About 2 tablespoons
    ice-cold water

FOR THE FILLING
450g (1lb) young rhubarb
25g (1oz) plain flour
About 115g (4oz) caster sugar
Grated rind of 1 orange
1 egg, beaten
4 tablespoons orange juice
Milk and caster sugar, for glazing

Serves 6

Sieve the flour, salt and spice into a mixing bowl. Rub in the butter lightly until the mixture resembles breadcrumbs. Stir in the sugar and mix to a firm dough with the beaten egg and water. Roll out thinly and use to line a buttered 20cm (8in) flan tin or pie plate. Chill for 30 minutes, then bake blind in the usual way (see Taffety Tart, page 40).

Cut the rhubarb into short lengths and arrange in the chilled pastry case. Put the flour, sugar and orange rind in a small basin. Add the beaten egg and blend well until smooth. Heat the orange juice in a small saucepan until it reaches boiling point, then pour on the egg mixture gradually, stirring continuously. Return to the pan and bring to the boil again, stirring all the time. Pour over the rhubarb.

Roll the pastry trimmings into long strips 1cm (½in) wide and arrange in a lattice pattern over the top of the tart, twisting them like barley sugar, and sticking the ends down with a little water. Brush each strip with a little milk and sprinkle with sugar.

Bake in a preheated oven at 200°C, 400°F, gas mark 6 for 35–40 minutes, until the rhubarb is tender and the pastry lattice is golden. Serve warm or cold, with Vanilla Custard Sauce (see page 35) or thick cream.

ROYAL PYE

In Elizabethan times a 'royal pye' was any savoury or sweet pie that was 'iced' with sugar and egg white, more like modern royal icing than meringue, which is a descendant. This particular Royal Pye is filled with mincemeat, apples and grapes and is ideal for serving at Christmas alongside, or instead of, the plum pudding. The rich shortcrust pastry was originally called 'biscuit crust'.

175g (6oz) sweet shortcrust
    pastry (see Raspberry and
    Cream Tart, page 44)
450g (1lb) Cox's apples
115g (4oz) seedless green grapes
450g (1lb) homemade or good-
    quality mincemeat
1–2 tablespoons brandy
    or sherry
2 egg whites
115g (4oz) caster sugar

Serves 6–8

After making your pastry, chill in the refrigerator for 30 minutes, then roll out and use to line a buttered 23cm (9in) flan tin. Chill again for about 15 minutes. Preheat the oven to 200°C, 400°F, gas mark 6 and bake blind in the usual way (see Taffety Tart, page 40).

Peel, core and chop the apples. Halve the grapes if large. Mix the apples and grapes with the mincemeat, stir in the brandy or sherry, then spoon into the pastry case. Cook in the preheated oven at 190°C, 375°F, gas mark 5 for 30 minutes.

Whisk the egg whites until stiff and whisk in half the caster sugar until smooth and glossy. Gently fold in the remaining sugar and pile meringue on top of the pie. Put back in the oven and bake for a further 15–20 minutes until the meringue is crisp and lightly brown. Serve warm with cream or a hard sauce (see page 55).

VARIATION
ALMOND ROYAL PYE
Use almond pastry instead of a rich shortcrust – 225g (8oz) plain flour, 115g (4oz) butter, 25g (1oz) caster sugar, 25g (1oz) ground almonds and 3 tablespoons ice-cold water.

MUCKY MOUTH PIE

A traditional fruit pie from the north of England made with apples, bilberries and fresh mint. For many centuries the latter was thought to be aphrodisiac, but who knows whether northern housewives were aware of this? Certainly this pie was a favourite with their menfolk.

The pastry lid is 'iced' in the traditional way, so the fruit needs to be on the sharp side. If you don't want to use bilberries, blackcurrants, blackberries, blueberries or damsons are all suitable.

225g (8oz) shortcrust pastry
   (see page 10)

FOR THE FILLING
2 large Bramley apples
450g (1lb) bilberries
2 tablespoons fresh mint,
   finely chopped
A little caster sugar

FOR THE ICING
115g (4oz) icing sugar
1 large egg white

Serves 6

Chill the pastry, then roll out half of it and use to line a buttered 20cm (8in) pie plate or flan ring. Prick the base of the pastry, then chill again.

Peel, core and slice the apples and cook them to a purée with a very little water. Mix with the bilberries and chopped mint. Sprinkle with a little sugar – not too much because of the sweet icing on top of the pie. Spoon the fruit mixture into the flan ring or pie plate and roll out the rest of the pastry to make a lid. Bake in a preheated oven at 200°C, 400°F, gas mark 6 for about 25 minutes, then remove from the oven and leave to cool slightly. Reduce the oven temperature to 180°C, 350°F, gas mark 4.

To prepare the icing, whisk the egg white until very stiff, then whisk in the sieved icing sugar until the mixture stands in peaks. Spread thickly over the pie crust and put back in the oven for about 10 minutes, until the icing hardens and is very slightly browned.

Serve warm with cream.

Right: Mucky Mouth Pie
Next page: Royal Pie

GYPSY TART

An almost forgotten 20th-century classic, this delicious butterscotch tart originated from Kent. If you were at school in the 1950s and 60s you will remember it with affection and it's well worth reviving. Children still love it. I have included nuts in this recipe, to make it more grown-up, but omit them if you want to taste the original.

FOR THE PASTRY
225g (8oz) plain flour
115g (4oz) butter
Cold water to mix

FOR THE FILLING
400g (14oz) tin evaporated milk,
  chilled overnight
350g (12oz) dark muscovado
  sugar
Chopped walnuts or pecan nuts
  (optional)
Sifted icing sugar, for dusting

Serves 8

To make the pastry, sieve the flour into a mixing bowl, then rub in the butter until the mixture resembles fine breadcrumbs. Add 2–4 tablespoons of cold water and mix to a dough. Knead lightly, then leave to rest for at least 10 minutes in the refrigerator. Preheat the oven to 200°C, 400°F, gas mark 6 with a large baking sheet in the oven to heat up as well.

Roll the pastry out and line a deep, buttered 25cm (10in) loose-bottomed flan tin. Bake blind in the usual way (see Taffety Tart, page 40).

Meanwhile, whisk the evaporated milk and sugar with an electric whisk for about 15 minutes.

Remove the baking sheet with the pastry case from the oven. Pour the filling into the pastry case and scatter over the chopped nuts, if using.

Return to the centre of the oven and bake for a further 10 minutes (the filling will still be slightly wobbly but will set on cooling). Remove from the oven and leave to cool until just warm.

Serve dusted with icing sugar and with pouring cream.

Left: Gypsy Tart
Previous page: Lady's Tart

LADY'S TART

This 19th-century tart was originally filled with apricot preserve and decorated with flaked almonds.
It had a decorative edge of small pastry circles. In this recipe, I have used four varieties of jam laid in sections and
divided by strips of pastry – once the pride of housewives, who, of course, used their best homemade jams.

225g (8oz) shortcrust pastry
   (see page 10)
2 tablespoons apricot jam
2 tablespoons raspberry or
   strawberry jam
2 tablespoons blackcurrant jam
2 tablespoons green gooseberry
   or greengage jam
Milk or water, for brushing
1 egg, beaten
1 tablespoon cold water

Serves 6

Roll out the pastry thinly and use two-thirds of it to line a buttered 25cm (10in) ovenproof plate. Divide the pastry base into 8 sections, marking lightly with a knife. Spread each section with a different jam, alternating the colours and avoiding the rim of the plate. Cut the pastry trimmings into narrow strips and arrange in twists across the tart, dividing the jams.

Cut the remaining one-third of the pastry into small circles with a 2.5cm (1in) cutter.

Brush the rim of the pastry-lined plate with a little milk or water and arrange the circles around the edge, overlapping them a little.

Beat the egg with the water and brush the pastry circles and twists carefully to glaze. Bake in the centre of a preheated oven at 190°C, 375°F, gas mark 5 for about 30 minutes or until the pastry is golden brown. Serve hot or cold with Vanilla Custard Sauce (see page 35) or with thick cream.

TREACLE TART

With the setting up of sugar refineries in British ports in the late 18th century, treacle, the syrup remaining after the sugar had been refined, was generally available. The origin of treacle tart may be medieval gingerbread, which was made by pressing breadcrumbs, treacle, spices and colourings together. Treacle was later replaced in tarts by golden syrup, but the name remained. In the north it continued to be popular as it was a cheaper sweetener.

175g (6oz) shortcrust pastry
   (see page 10)
50g (1¾oz) fresh white
   breadcrumbs
grated rind and juice of 1 lemon
½ teaspoon ground ginger
6 tablespoons golden syrup
3 tablespoons double cream

Serves 6

Preheat the oven to 200°C, 400°F, gas mark 6, with a large baking sheet in the oven to warm up as well. Chill the pastry, then roll out thinly and use to line a buttered 20cm (8in) shallow loose-bottomed flan tin. Bake blind in the usual way (see Taffety Tart, page 40). Remove from the oven and cool briefly.

Mix the filling ingredients together and pour into the pastry case. Bake in the preheated oven for 5 minutes, then reduce to 170°C, 325°F, gas mark 3. Bake for a further 25 minutes, or until golden brown and set.

Remove from the oven and leave to cool for at least 30 minutes, then serve warm with Vanilla Custard Sauce (see page 35), ice cream or cream.

CHERRY AND BRANDY DISH PIE

Cherry pies and 'bumpers', or pasties, were baked and eaten at cherry-pie feasts to celebrate the harvesting of the fruit, in the principal cherry-growing areas of England, such as Kent and Buckinghamshire.

FOR THE PASTRY
225g (8oz) plain flour
Pinch of salt
115g (4oz) butter
25g (1oz) caster sugar
1 egg yolk
About 2 tablespoons
    ice-cold water

FOR THE FILLING
900g (2lb) stoned cherries
About 115g (4oz) caster sugar
Knob of butter
Milk and caster sugar, for glazing
2 tablespoons cherry brandy
    or brandy
3 tablespoons double cream

Serves 6

Sieve the flour and salt together into a mixing bowl. Rub in the butter until the mixture resembles breadcrumbs. Stir in the caster sugar, egg yolk and enough cold water to mix to a firm dough. Knead lightly until smooth and chill for at least 30 minutes. Fill an 850ml (1½ pint) pie dish with stoned cherries, sprinkle with sugar and dot with butter.

Roll out the pastry on a lightly floured board and cover the dish of cherries. Flute the edges of the pastry lid and make a couple of slits in the top to let out the steam. Decorate with pastry trimmings. Brush with milk and caster sugar. Bake in the centre of a preheated oven at 200°C, 400°F, gas mark 6 for 20 minutes, then reduce the heat to 180°C, 350°F, gas mark 4 and continue cooking for 20–25 minutes or until the pastry is golden brown.

Remove from the oven and cut neatly round the lid of the pie. Lift off carefully, and pour cherry brandy or brandy and cream over the fruit. Replace the pastry lid, dust with extra caster sugar and return to the oven for 5 minutes. Serve hot with whipped or clotted cream.

SUMMER FRUIT AND BRANDY PIE

If you don't live in an area where cherries are readily available in season, you may like to take advantage of the fruits that are grown locally, such as raspberries or blackcurrants. This variation of the Cherry and Brandy Dish Pie uses three summer fruits, but you can use just one, two or a different combination as desired.

ALTERNATIVE INGREDIENTS:
450g (1lb) raspberries
225g (8oz) blackcurrants
225g (8oz) redcurrants
2 tablespoons brandy

Make the pie in the same way as the Cherry and Brandy Dish Pie opposite, but using a combination of soft summer fruits – raspberries, blackcurrants and redcurrants – instead of cherries. Use brandy instead of cherry brandy. Serve with whipped or clotted cream.

CUMBERLAND RUM NICKY

Small versions of this pie, similar to mince pies and called Rum Nickies, can also be made. It recalls the days in the 18th century when Whitehaven in Cumbria was one of the leading ports in the rum trade with the West Indies.

FOR THE PASTRY
225g (8oz) plain flour
Pinch of salt
115g (4oz) butter
25g (1oz) caster sugar
1 egg yolk
2–3 tablespoons ice-cold water

FOR THE FILLING
115g (4oz) chopped dates
50g (1¾oz) chopped
    preserved ginger
50g (1¾oz) butter
25g (1oz) caster sugar
2 tablespoons dark rum
Icing sugar for dusting

Serves 6

Sieve the flour and salt together into a mixing bowl. Rub in the butter until the mixture resembles breadcrumbs. Stir in the sugar. Add the egg yolk and enough ice-cold water to mix to a firm dough. Knead lightly until smooth. Chill for at least 30 minutes.

Roll out the pastry on a lightly floured board. Line a greased 20cm (8in) pie or ovenproof plate with half the pastry. Sprinkle over the chopped dates and ginger. Cream the butter and sugar together until pale and fluffy. Beat in the rum gradually. Spread the mixture over the fruit in the pie plate. Cover with the remaining pastry, sealing the edges well. Make a couple of slits in the top of the pastry, flute the edges and decorate as you wish with pastry trimmings. Bake in the centre of a preheated oven at 200°C, 400°F, gas mark 6 for 10–15 minutes and then reduce the temperature to 180°C, 350°F, gas mark 4 for a further 25–30 minutes. Serve hot, dusted with icing sugar and with whipped or clotted cream or a hard sauce such as Rum and Orange Butter (see opposite).

BRANDY AND LEMON BUTTER

This sauce is traditionally served at Christmas, but can be used to enliven many other puddings. It is a 'hard sauce':
these are cold sauces made by creaming butter with other flavourings, giving a buttery rather than a liquid
consistency.

115g (4oz) butter
115g (4oz) caster sugar
½ teaspoon grated lemon rind
1 tablespoon boiling water
1 teaspoon lemon juice
4 tablespoons brandy
Grated lemon rind for
    decoration

Cut the butter into small pieces and put with sugar and lemon rind in a warmed bowl. Beat until creamy. Add the boiling water and continue to beat until every grain of sugar has dissolved (this will prevent the sauce from developing a gritty texture). Add the lemon juice and brandy a little at a time, beating continuously to stop the sauce curdling. When the sauce is completely blended, put in an attractive dish and store in a refrigerator until needed.

VARIATIONS
Add a few chopped glacé cherries and angelica to the sauce, or a little chopped preserved stem ginger.

RUM AND ORANGE BUTTER
Make exactly as Brandy and Lemon Butter, substituting orange rind and juice for lemon, and rum for brandy. Serve chilled, sprinkled with grated orange rind.

SENIOR WRANGLER SAUCE
Cut the butter into small pieces and put with sugar in a warmed bowl. Beat until creamy. Add 50g (2oz) ground almonds and boiling water and continue to beat until every grain of sugar has dissolved. Gradually add brandy and a few drops of almond essence, beating continuously.

STOVE-TOP PUDDINGS

Fried puddings were some of the earliest puddings to be made, as the method was so simple and they could be cooked directly over the fire. Eggs were mixed with flour to make pancakes, although they were not considered important enough to be listed in recipe books. Some were made from egg whites only and these were much admired and served as fritters, sprinkled with sugar. These appeared regularly on medieval menus as part of the last course – apple, parsnip and carrot fritters were the most popular.

In Tudor and Stuart times, milk or water and spices were added to pancake batter, and the Georgians used cream as well as brandy to enrich the batter. Fritters continued to be popular, although again the batter was further enriched.

Heavy suet-pudding mixtures were also fried as an alternative to boiling. The method was much faster and easier. The mixture was formed into small cakes or balls and fried or stewed in butter.

The important thing to remember when cooking fried puddings is that the fat or butter must be at the right temperature, particularly when deep frying. Also, most must be prepared at the last minute, although if you have a freezer they can be frozen once cooked and reheated when ready to serve.

ELDERFLOWER FRITTERS

Make the batter just before you cook the fritters and eat piping hot. Pick the flowers on a sunny morning.

8 elderflower heads in perfect
    condition, each with 1cm
    (½in) of stalk
115g (4oz) self-raising flour
Fizzy water to mix
Sunflower oil for frying
Icing sugar, for dusting
Thick cream, for serving

Serves 4

Shake each elderflower head to remove any insects. Sieve the flour into a bowl and mix in enough water to make a batter the texture of single cream (about 200–250ml or 7–9fl oz). Heat about 2.5cm (1in) depth of sunflower oil in a pan until it sizzles when a drop of water is dropped in at arm's length. Working quickly, hold the stalk of a flower head and dip it into the batter. Lower it into the hot oil and fry until light golden. Remove from the pan and drain on kitchen paper. Serve immediately, dusted with icing sugar and with thick cream.

NEW COLLEGE PUDDINGS

Traditionally served at New College, Oxford, in the 19th century, these first appeared in a recipe book by Dr William Kitchiner, published in 1831. They were basically suet puddings that were fried instead of boiled, reducing the cooking time considerably. Oxford Dumplings were very similar.

115g (4oz) suet
115g (4oz) fresh white
    breadcrumbs
50g (1¾oz) caster or
    soft brown sugar
15g (½oz) baking powder
Pinch of salt
½ teaspoon grated nutmeg
Grated rind of 1 orange
115g (4oz) currants
25g (1oz) candied peel
3 eggs, separated
2 tablespoons brandy (optional)
Butter, for frying

Serves 6

Mix the suet, breadcrumbs, sugar, baking powder, salt and nutmeg with orange rind, currants and candied peel, stirring thoroughly. Beat the egg yolks and mix with brandy, if using. Stir into the pudding mixture. Whisk the egg whites and gently fold into the pudding, which should be a soft dropping consistency. Melt some butter in a heavy frying pan and fry tablespoonfuls of pudding mixture in hot butter, flattening the mixture as you cook it (like a fish cake). Turn once, frying each side for about 6 minutes until brown. Serve hot, sprinkled with sugar, and with Vanilla Custard Sauce (see page 35).

SWEET APPLE OMELET

The sweet omelet was very popular in Edwardian times and was often served as a country-weekend treat, when the cook would prepare it while the guests were eating the main course. It would then be brought to the table, flaming with brandy or rum. In this recipe the omelet is filled with apples, but you can use cherries, plums or apricots in the same way or just serve filled with jam, which is the traditional way. Apricot jam was always used.

2 large cooking apples
115g (4oz) butter
115g (4oz) caster sugar
2 tablespoons apple brandy
    or rum
150ml (¼ pint) double
    or whipping cream
5 eggs
Pinch of salt

Serves 4

Peel, core and slice the apples. Fry them gently in 50g (1¾oz) butter, turning frequently until tender. Remove from the heat and add 50g (1¾oz) caster sugar, the apple brandy and the double or whipping cream. Stir well.

Separate 2 of the eggs and beat the egg yolks and 3 whole eggs together. Add salt and 25g (1oz) caster sugar. Whisk the 2 egg whites until stiff and gently fold into the egg mixture.

In a frying pan melt the remaining butter. When light brown in colour, pour in the egg mixture and cook over a moderate heat, mixing it well with a fork to allow the uncooked egg to run on to the bottom of the hot pan. Cook until golden brown on the bottom and cooked on the top (sweet omelets, unlike savoury omelets, should not be runny on the top). Spread the apple mixture over the top, fold in half and slide on to a warmed plate. Sprinkle with the remaining caster sugar and caramelize by placing the omelet under a very hot grill for a few minutes.

Another attractive way of finishing this omelet is to heat a skewer until it is red hot and then draw it over the top of the sugar-sprinkled omelet in a criss-cross pattern.

PUFFED STRAWBERRY OMELET

A fluffy sweet omelet flavoured with orange rind and orange-flower water and filled with fresh strawberries. This kind of omelet was known as a popular treat over a hundred years ago.

3 eggs, separated
2 level teaspoons caster sugar
Grated rind of 1 orange
½ teaspoon orange-flower
    water (optional)
2 tablespoons water
15g (½oz) butter
225g (8oz) sliced strawberries
25g (1oz) icing sugar, sifted
1 tablespoon Grand Marnier
    (optional)

Serves 2

Whisk the egg whites with caster sugar until stiff, but not dry. Beat the egg yolks, orange rind, orange-flower water, if using, and water until creamy. Melt the butter in an omelet pan or small frying pan over a low heat. Fold the egg whites carefully into the yolks using a metal spoon. Be careful not to overmix. Tip the omelet pan to coat the sides with butter. Pour in the egg mixture. Cook over a moderate heat until golden brown underneath and just firm to the touch in the centre. Place under a pre-heated grill and cook until just set. Spread with sliced strawberries and sprinkle with sifted icing sugar. Fold the omelet and slide gently on to a hot serving plate. Dust with more icing sugar. Warm the Grand Marnier, if using, in a small saucepan, pour over the omelet and set alight. Take to the table immediately, while the omelet is still flaming. Serve with sweetened whipped cream.

VARIATION

A PUFFED LEMON OMELET

Replace 1 tablespoon of the water with lemon juice, and use grated lemon rind instead of orange. Omit the orange-flower water and add a little more caster sugar. Serve without the strawberry filling. Set alight with brandy if you like.

POOR KNIGHTS OF WINDSOR

A traditional pudding from Berkshire – where the alleged poverty of medieval knights was jokingly commemorated – consisting of bread, soaked in sherry or wine, eggs and cream, and fried. The recipe probably originated from France, where it was called Pain Perdu *or 'Lost Bread'. It is an excellent way of using up leftover bread or rolls. Also known in Georgian times as Spanish Fritters.*

6 thick slices of white bread
2 eggs
2 teaspoons caster sugar
150ml (¼ pint) single cream
　or milk
Pinch of ground cinnamon
Grated rind of ½ lemon
2 tablespoons Madeira
　or sweet sherry
Butter and oil for frying
Extra caster sugar and cinnamon,
　for sprinkling
Orange or lemon wedges,
　for serving

Serves 6

Remove the crusts from the bread and cut each slice into 3 fingers. Beat the eggs and sugar together in a basin. Heat the cream or milk until it just reaches boiling point. Cool a little before pouring on to the egg mixture, beating continuously. Stir in cinnamon, lemon rind and Madeira or sherry.

　Melt a little butter and oil in a heavy frying pan. Dip each finger or piece of bread into the custard mixture and fry until golden brown and crisp. Drain on crumpled kitchen paper and keep warm until all the bread has been fried. Sprinkle with caster sugar and ground cinnamon. Serve with orange or lemon wedges.

VARIATION
EGGY BREAD WITH MAPLE FRIED APPLES
Melt 15g (½oz) butter in a frying pan and add 2 crisp dessert apples, unpeeled, cored and thickly sliced, 1 tablespoon of pure maple syrup and a generous pinch of ground cinnamon. Cook over a medium heat for about 10 minutes until the apples are just tender. Cook the pudding as before, then serve the fingers of fried bread topped with the apples and pan juices. Serve with thick cream if you wish.

TRADITIONAL LEMON PANCAKES

Although probably not of British origin, pancakes have been established here for so many centuries that they may be considered a national institution. When Lent was strictly observed, eggs and fatty foods were forbidden for forty days and so pancake-making became associated with Shrove Tuesday in the UK, to use up any remaining eggs, butter and milk before the fasting.

115g (4oz) plain flour
Pinch of salt
Grated rind of 1 lemon
1 egg
300ml (½ pint) milk
15g (½oz) melted butter
Butter, for frying
Caster sugar, for sprinkling
2 lemons, for serving

Makes about 10 pancakes

Sieve the flour and salt together into a basin. Stir in the lemon rind. Make a well in the centre and break in the egg. Beat well, incorporating the flour, and add half the liquid very gradually, beating all the time until a smooth batter is formed. Add the remaining liquid a little at a time and beat until well mixed. Leave to stand for at least 30 minutes.

Stir melted butter into the batter just before cooking. Heat a very little butter in a pancake or omelet pan until very hot. Spoon in a tablespoon of batter and tip the pan until the batter covers its base. Cook until golden brown underneath. Turn over with a palette knife and cook the other side until golden. Turn out on to sugared greaseproof paper and sprinkle with caster sugar and a squeeze of lemon juice. Serve immediately with extra sugar and lemon wedges, or keep warm in the oven until needed.

VARIATIONS
ORANGE PANCAKES
Add the grated rind of 2 oranges to the batter before cooking. To serve, sprinkle with sugar and pour orange juice over the pancakes.

CARAMELIZED APPLE PANCAKES
Fill the cooked pancakes with apple slices sautéed in a little butter. Fold over and sprinkle generously with caster or icing sugar. Place under a hot grill just long enough to crisp the pancakes and glaze the sugar.

APPLE FRITTERS

Egg-batter fritters have been popular since medieval days. The most common fritters in Britain were made with apples, although later oranges, pineapple, bananas and pieces of pumpkin became popular.

115g (4oz) plain flour
Pinch of salt
½ teaspoon ground cinnamon
150ml (¼ pint) tepid water
2 tablespoons orange liqueur
1 tablespoon vegetable oil
4 medium cooking or crisp
   dessert apples
Grated rind and juice of ½ lemon
50g (1¾oz) icing sugar
25g (1oz) caster sugar
6 tablespoons apricot jam or
   thick orange marmalade
2 tablespoons water
Fat for deep frying (lard or oil)
2 egg whites
Caster sugar for dusting
Orange or lemon segments, for
   serving

Serves 6

Right: Apple Fritters

Sieve the flour, salt and cinnamon together into a basin. Make a well in the centre. Gradually blend in the water and 1 tablespoon of liqueur, followed by oil. Beat with a rotary or electric whisk to make a glossy batter. Cover and leave to stand in a cool place for at least 30 minutes.

Peel, core and slice the apples in 6mm (¼in) thick slices. Mix together the lemon rind and juice, 1 tablespoon liqueur and sieved icing sugar. Add the apple slices and coat evenly. In a heavy saucepan, dissolve the caster sugar and jam over a low heat. Dilute with water to make a syrup of coating consistency. Simmer the syrup for 1 minute and keep warm. Coat each soaked apple ring in this syrup, allowing the excess to drain off. Leave the apple rings on one side to dry a little.

Heat the fat for deep frying to 190°C, 375°F, gas mark 5. When a blue vapour rises from the fat, it is hot enough. Test by dropping in a little batter, which will rise if the fat is the correct temperature; if not, the batter will sink. Make sure your fat is clean and at least 7.5cm (3in) deep. Whisk the egg whites until very stiff and fold into the prepared batter. Using cooking tongs or a long skewer, dip the apple rings, one at a time, into the batter, allowing the excess to drain off. Lower carefully into the hot fat and deep-fry until crisp and puffed, turning them over once or twice. Avoid frying too many at once, because this cools the fat and does not allow room for the fritters to expand properly. When cooked, remove from fat and drain on crumpled kitchen paper. Serve immediately dusted with caster sugar.

A QUIRE OF PAPER

Much admired by 17th- and 18th-century cooks, a quire of paper consisted of a pile of wafer-thin pancakes. The batter, rich with eggs and cream, was run as thinly as possible over the bottom of a heavy pan and cooked on one side only. The completed pancakes were dusted with caster sugar and laid evenly one upon another until the pile contained twenty. A wine sauce and melted butter were served with the pancakes, which were cut into wedges like a cake.

115g (4oz) plain flour
Pinch of salt
25g (1oz) caster sugar
2 eggs
2 egg yolks
2 tablespoons medium sherry
   or Madeira
Unsalted butter for frying
300ml (½ pint) single cream
   or half cream and milk
Caster sugar, for sprinkling

Serves 6

Sieve the flour and salt together into a basin. Stir in the sugar. Make a well in the centre of the flour. Put the eggs and egg yolks into the well and gradually mix the eggs and flour together. Add cream (or cream and milk) gradually, beating well until a smooth batter is formed. Stir in the sherry or Madeira to make a thin cream.

Heat a heavy-based pancake or omelet pan, brush with melted butter and add 1 tablespoon of batter. Twist the pan until the bottom is evenly coated with batter and cook until the pancake is golden brown on the bottom. Remove from the pan or turn over and cook the other side. Keep warm in a clean tea towel. Make a stack of pancakes, filling them with jam and whipped cream or whatever you choose. Sprinkle liberally with caster sugar.

Serve hot, cut in wedges with Eliza Acton's Madeira Sauce (see page 67).

Left: A Quire of Paper

DURHAM FLUFFIN'

A milk pudding traditionally eaten in the north-east of England on Christmas Eve. The pearl barley has to be soaked in water overnight.

2 tablespoons pearl barley,
   soaked overnight in water
600ml (1 pint) full-cream milk
¾ teaspoon grated nutmeg
A few drops of brandy
50g (1¾oz) soft brown sugar or
   1 tablespoon honey
Crystallized orange slices and
   pouring cream for decorating

Serves 6

Simmer the soaked pearl barley in the milk for about 30 minutes or until it is a smooth cream. Add grated nutmeg, brandy, and sugar or honey to taste. Serve hot in individual dishes with plenty of pouring cream, decorated with crystallized orange slices or with cream and Jam Sauce (see opposite).

JAM SAUCE

This simple sauce is good with many hot, creamy puddings, or with sponges such as The Duchess's Pudding (see page 81).

3 tablespoons raspberry, strawberry, plum, apricot or blackcurrant jam
6 tablespoons water
1 teaspoon lemon juice

Melt the jam in a saucepan with water and lemon juice. Push through a sieve to make a smooth sauce. Serve hot.

ELIZA ACTON'S MADEIRA SAUCE

This sauce, from Eliza Acton's 1845 cookbook, is delicious drizzled over a stack of pancakes.

Finely pared rind of ½ lemon
150ml (¼ pint) water
50g (1 ¾ oz) soft brown sugar
25g (1oz) butter
2 level teaspoons cornflour
150ml (¼ pint) Madeira or sweet sherry

Simmer the lemon rind, water and sugar in a saucepan for 10–15 minutes. Strain to remove the lemon rind. Return the syrup to the saucepan. Work the butter and cornflour together in a small basin. Add small pieces of this creamed mixture to the hot syrup to thicken. Add Madeira or sherry, and reheat, but don't boil. Serve hot in a warmed sauceboat.

STEAMED AND BOILED PUDDINGS

The ancestor of the boiled pudding was the medieval 'pottage', a kind of porridge of cereal, honey, wild fruits and shredded meat or fish. Later, in Tudor and Stuart times, meatless puddings of breadcrumbs, rice or oatmeal were mixed with milk, cream, eggs, spices and dried fruit, stuffed into animal guts and boiled. They were then removed from the guts and browned in front of the fire, and served sprinkled with sugar and melted butter. Although animal guts were useful as containers for boiling puddings, they had several disadvantages, because they were awkward to clean, inconvenient to fill and, of course, were only available at pig- or sheep-killing time. Experiments were made using other containers such as hollowed turnips, carrots and cucumbers. This practice continued all through the 17th century, but did not lead to any real development in pudding-making.

The future of the boiled suet pudding as one of England's national dishes was assured only when the pudding cloth came into use. It received one of its earliest mentions in a recipe for College Pudding or Cambridge Pudding dated 1617. The invention of the pudding cloth or bag firmly cut the link between puddings and animal guts. Puddings could now be made at any time and they became a regular part of the daily fare of almost all classes. One of the advantages of a pudding wrapped in its pudding cloth was that it could be simmered along with the meat by the poorer housewife, whose principal means of cooking in the 17th century was still a cauldron suspended from a pot-hook over the fire.

Suet was sometimes replaced by bone marrow in boiled puddings. Ground almonds were often an ingredient and dried fruit was added liberally in some recipes to make a 'plum' pudding. It was found that dried fruit did not lose its flavour and consistency as much as fresh fruit, although before the end of the 17th century the boiled pudding, composed of a suet crust wrapped around a filling of apples or gooseberries, had come into existence. Mace, nutmeg, cinnamon and ginger were spices commonly used for seasoning. Heavy suet boiled puddings reached their peak of popularity in Victorian times, when they were much loved by Prince Albert. He was responsible for introducing the 'plum pudding' as part of traditional Christmas fare.

BACHELOR'S PUDDING

A lovely light steamed pudding from Mrs Beeton, which is typically Victorian in character and would have been served for lunch, or as a filler for the servants' main meal at midday.

2 tablespoons golden syrup

115g (4oz) unsalted butter

115g (4oz) caster sugar

2 eggs

140g (5oz) self-raising flour

2 tablespoons milk or water

450g (1lb) cooking apples

50g (1¾oz) currants

85g (3oz) demerara sugar

1 level teaspoon ground
   cinnamon

Serves 6

Butter thoroughly a 1.2 litre (2 pint) pudding basin. Pour the golden syrup into the bottom. Cream the butter and caster sugar together until pale and fluffy. Beat the eggs and add gradually to the creamed mixture. Fold in the flour gently with a metal spoon. Add sufficient milk or water to make a soft dropping consistency. Peel, core and slice the apples and mix with currants, demerara sugar and cinnamon. Pour a layer of the pudding mixture into the bottom of the prepared basin, top with a layer of apple mixture, then another layer of pudding mixture and then the remaining apples. Spoon over the remaining pudding mixture. Cover securely and steam for 2–2½ hours until firm and well risen. Turn out on to a warm serving dish and serve with clotted cream or Vanilla Custard Sauce (see page 35).

APPLE HAT

A favourite Victorian suet-crust pudding filled with juicy apples, raisins and spices. Other seasonal fruits are just as successful – try pears, plums, damsons, greengages, rhubarb or gooseberries. The dried fruit can be omitted, chopped nuts added and alternative spices used.

225g (8oz) self-raising flour
Pinch of salt
115g (4oz) suet
6–8 tablespoons cold water
675g (1½lb) cooking apples
50g (1¾oz) raisins or sultanas
85g (3oz) brown or white sugar
3 cloves
Pinch of ground cinnamon
Pinch of ground ginger
Grated rind and juice of
    ½ lemon or 1 orange
50g (1¾oz) unsalted butter
1 tablespoon clotted cream

Serves 6

Sieve the flour with salt into a mixing bowl. Stir in the suet and mix with sufficient cold water to make a soft, light dough. Knead lightly and roll out on a floured board about 6mm (¼in) thick. Use two-thirds of the pastry to line a prepared 1.2 litre (2 pint) pudding basin.

Peel, core and slice the apples and fill the lined basin with layers of apples, raisins or sultanas, sugar and spices. Add lemon or orange rind and juice and the butter, cut into small pieces. Cover the basin with the reserved piece of pastry, dampening the edges and pressing together firmly. Cover securely and steam for 2–2½ hours.

Turn out on to a warm serving plate and remove a square of the pastry from the top of the pudding. Pop in a tablespoon of clotted cream, which will melt into the pudding. Serve hot with Vanilla Custard Sauce (see page 35).

VARIATIONS

APPLE AND BRAMBLE HAT
Use 450g (1lb) cooking apples and 225g (8oz) blackberries. Omit the raisins.

APPLE AND MARMALADE HAT
Replace the grated rind and juice of the lemon with 1–2 tablespoons orange or quince marmalade, and omit the raisins.

ORANGE AND TREACLE SPONGE PUDDING

Another very light sponge pudding, which has its own delicious sauce when turned out. It makes a fantastic 'dinner' pud when served with Orange Cream Sauce.

FOR THE SAUCE
3 tablespoons golden syrup
Grated rind and juice of 2 oranges
2 tablespoons fresh white
    breadcrumbs

FOR THE SPONGE
115g (4oz) unsalted butter
115g (4oz) caster sugar
2 eggs
115g (4oz) self-raising flour
About 1 tablespoon cold water

FOR THE ORANGE CREAM
    SAUCE
600ml (1 pint) double cream
1 tablespoon caster sugar
Grated rind and juice of 2 oranges

Serves 6

Butter an 850ml (1½ pint) pudding basin thoroughly. Put golden syrup, the rind of 1 orange, and the juice of 2 oranges into a small, heavy saucepan. Warm gently to make a runny sauce. Fold in the breadcrumbs and pour the sauce into the bottom of the prepared basin.

Cream the butter and sugar together until pale and fluffy. Beat the eggs and add a little at a time to the creamed mixture. Sieve the flour and gently fold into the mixture using a metal spoon. Stir in the rind of the second orange and enough water to make a soft dropping consistency. Pour the mixture into the prepared basin and cover securely. Steam for 1½–2 hours until well risen and firm.

Turn out on to a large warm serving plate, allowing room for the sauce. Serve with Orange Cream Sauce (see below), Vanilla Custard Sauce (see page 35) or cream.

ORANGE CREAM SAUCE
Simmer the cream and sugar together in a large saucepan for about 45 minutes, or until it has reduced by half. Stir in the orange rind and juice and serve.

Right: Orange and Treacle Sponge Pudding
Next page: Apple Hat

SPOTTED DICK

Setting aside the double entendre, the contentious word is thought to be a Huddersfield term for pudding.
A Spotted Dick is traditionally made with currants only, but use raisins or a mixture of dried fruits if you wish.

225g (8oz) self-raising flour
Pinch of salt
115g (4oz) suet, butter or
  margarine
25g (1oz) caster sugar
175g (6oz) currants, soaked
  in brandy
About 150ml (¼ pint)
  full-cream milk

Serves 6

Butter a 1.2 litre (2 pint) pudding basin. Sieve together the flour and salt into the basin, then stir in the suet, or rub in the butter or margarine. Add sugar and soaked currants. Mix with enough milk to make a soft dropping consistency. Turn into the basin and cover securely. Steam for 2 hours, then serve very hot with Vanilla Custard, Lemon or Syrup Sauce (see pages 35, 81 and 94).

VARIATION
GINGER SPOTTED DICK
Sieve ½ teaspoon ground ginger with flour and salt and add 2 pieces of finely chopped preserved ginger to the currants.

Left: Spotted Dick
Previous page: Rich Chocolate Pudding

RICH CHOCOLATE PUDDING

A deliciously light steamed chocolate pudding with a soufflé-like texture. Breadcrumbs are used instead of flour to give the light result.

85g (3oz) good-quality plain chocolate
50g (1¾oz) butter
300ml (½ pint) full-cream milk
50g (1¾oz) caster sugar
2 eggs, separated
½ teaspoon vanilla essence
150g (5½oz) fresh white breadcrumbs

Serves 6

Butter an 850ml (1½ pint) pudding basin well. Melt the chocolate and butter in a basin over a saucepan of hot water (don't be tempted to use cooking chocolate for this pudding – the flavour will not be as good). Remove the chocolate from the heat and stir. Warm the milk in a saucepan and add gradually to the chocolate mixture. Stir in the sugar. Beat the egg yolks and add the vanilla essence. Stir into the chocolate mixture. Add the breadcrumbs. Whisk the egg whites until stiff and fold gently into the pudding mixture. Turn into the prepared basin and cover securely. Steam for 1½–2 hours until well risen and springy. Serve hot with Chocolate Orange or Chocolate and Coffee Sauce (see pages 94 and 95) or cold with whipped cream.

VARIATIONS

RICH CHOCOLATE AND WALNUT PUDDING
Add 85g (3oz) finely chopped walnuts.

RICH CHOCOLATE AND ORANGE PUDDING
Add grated rind of 1 orange and ½ lemon and 1 tablespoon brandy.

SUSSEX POND PUDDING

Kent and Sussex extend their rivalry to puddings – Kentish Well Pudding consists of a suet crust enclosing butter, brown sugar, currants and a whole lemon, while in Sussex Pond Pudding the currants are omitted. Either way, when the pudding is cut open, a rich sweet syrup – the well or pond – oozes out.

175g (6oz) self-raising flour
Pinch of salt
1 level teaspoon baking powder
50g (1¾oz) fresh white
  breadcrumbs
115g (4oz) suet
150ml (¼ pint) milk or a little
  more mixed cold milk and
  water
175g (6oz) butter
175g (6oz) demerara sugar
1 large thin-skinned lemon

Serves 6

Sift the flour, salt and baking powder into a mixing bowl. Stir in the breadcrumbs and suet. With a round-bladed knife, mix in the milk and water until you have a soft, elastic dough. Form the dough into a ball on a floured board. Generously butter a 1.2 litre (2 pint) pudding basin. Cut off a quarter of the dough and set aside for the lid. Roll out the large piece of dough into a circle about 5cm (2in) wider than the top of the pudding basin and line the basin with this pastry, pressing it to shape.

Cut the butter into rough pieces and put half of it with half the sugar into the pastry-lined basin. Prick the lemon deeply all over with a skewer and lay it on the butter and sugar. Then put the remaining butter and sugar on top. If the mixture is far below the top of the basin you can add some more butter and sugar. Fold the ends of the pastry in over the filling and moisten. Roll out the remaining pastry into a circle to form the lid and lay it on top, pressing the edge to seal. Cover securely and steam for 3½–4 hours, topping up with boiling water if necessary. Turn the pudding out on to a serving dish large enough for the juices to seep out round it. Serve hot with Vanilla Custard Sauce (see page 35) or cream.

VARIATION
KENTISH WELL PUDDING
Pack 115g (4oz) currants around the lemon and continue as before.

STEAMED LEMON CURD PUDDING

Citrus fruits began to arrive in Britain in the 13th century from the Mediterranean – lemons, oranges, which were of the bitter Seville type, and a few pomegranates. By the end of the Tudor period, lemons were being imported in large quantities and used in perfumes as well as for flavouring food. They have continued in popularity over the centuries. This pudding is very light and a refreshing end to a rich meal.

1 slice lemon

1 rounded tablespoon
   homemade or good-quality
   purchased lemon curd

115g (4oz) unsalted butter

115g (4oz) caster sugar

2 large eggs

Grated rind of 2 lemons

140g (5oz) self-raising flour

Pinch of salt

1 level teaspoon baking powder

3 tablespoons lemon juice

Serves 6

Butter a 1.2 litre (2 pint) pudding basin thoroughly. Place a slice of lemon in the bottom of the basin and cover it with lemon curd. Cream the butter and sugar together until pale and fluffy. Beat the eggs then beat into the mixture a little at a time. Add the lemon rind. Sieve the flour, salt and baking powder together and gradually fold into the creamed mixture. Mix to a soft dropping consistency with the lemon juice. Spoon the mixture into the prepared basin. Cover with a piece of buttered foil, making a pleat across the top of the basin. Cover securely, then steam for 1½–2 hours until well risen and firm.

Turn out the pudding on to a hot plate – and don't leave the lovely lemony topping behind in the basin! Serve hot with Vanilla Custard or Lemon Sauce (see pages 35 and 81).

VARIATION
STEAMED ORANGE CURD PUDDING
Use sweet or Seville oranges and orange curd instead of lemons.

STEAMED LEMON AND VANILLA SYRUP SPONGE

Another light steamed sponge pudding with a wonderful lemony sauce.

FOR THE SYRUP
Grated rind and juice of
  2 thin-skinned lemons
200g (7oz) caster sugar
150ml (¼ pint) water
1 vanilla pod

FOR THE SPONGE
175g (6oz) unsalted butter
150g (5½oz) caster sugar
1 thin-skinned lemon
3 eggs, beaten
200g (7oz) plain flour
1½ level teaspoons
  baking powder
3–4 tablespoons full-cream milk

Serves 6

To make the syrup, pour the lemon juice into a small saucepan with the lemon rind, caster sugar and water. Split the vanilla pod in half lengthways and scrape out the seeds, reserving them for later use. Add the pod to the saucepan and bring to the boil. Simmer until a syrupy consistency is achieved, then reserve.

For the sponge, cream together the butter and sugar with the rind from the lemon and the reserved vanilla seeds until light and fluffy. Gradually add the beaten eggs, then sieve in the flour and baking powder. Add enough milk to make a soft dropping consistency.

Butter a 1.2 litre (2 pint) pudding basin. Cut the zested lemon in half and trim off the top or bottom. Place one of the halves in the bottom of the basin, widest end downwards. Use the other half as you wish. Pour over the reserved syrup, saving a little for later. Carefully spoon the sponge batter into the basin, then cover securely. Steam for about 2 hours, until well risen and firm.

Turn out on to a warm serving plate and pour over the remaining syrup. Serve with chilled double cream.

CANARY PUDDING

This is one of the basic British light steamed puddings. In the past it would have been made of suet and boiled for at least three hours. Later, it was adapted and given a spongy texture, which is much lighter and easier on the stomach. It can be cooked in individual small moulds or darioles and called Castle Puddings or Sutherland Puddings. It was called Canary Pudding because originally it was made with a flavouring of Madeira, the sweet sherry-like fortified wine from the Canary Islands.

115g (4oz) unsalted butter
115g (4oz) caster sugar
2 eggs
50g (1¾oz) self-raising flour
50g (1¾oz) fresh white
   breadcrumbs
Grated rind and juice of
   1 lemon
1–2 tablespoons Madeira or
   sweet sherry

Serves 6

Butter a 1.2 litre (2 pint) pudding basin thoroughly. Cream the butter and sugar together until pale and fluffy. Beat the eggs and add gradually to the creamed mixture, beating well between each addition. Sieve the flour and gently fold into the pudding mixture. Carefully stir in the breadcrumbs and lemon rind and mix to a soft dropping consistency with the lemon juice and Madeira or sherry. Spoon into the prepared basin, cover securely and steam for about 2–2½ hours or until well risen and spongy. Serve hot with Vanilla Custard Sauce, Eliza Acton's Madeira Sauce or Lemon Sauce (see pages 35, 67 and 81).

VARIATION
BLACK CAP CANARY PUDDING
Put 3 tablespoons blackcurrant jam in the bottom of the basin before filling with the pudding mixture.

BRIGADE PUDDING

This is a pudding popular in the north of England, consisting of alternate layers of suet pastry and mincemeat.

225g (8oz) self-raising flour
Generous pinch of salt
115g (4oz) suet
Grated rind of ½ lemon
6–8 tablespoons cold water
2 tablespoons golden syrup
225g (8oz) mincemeat

Serves 6

Butter a 1.2 litre (2 pint) pudding basin well. Sieve the flour and salt together into a mixing bowl, and stir in the suet and lemon rind. Add sufficient water to mix to a soft but not sticky dough. Turn on to a floured board and divide into 4 portions, each a little larger than the next. Spoon golden syrup into the bottom of the prepared basin. Pat the smallest portion of dough into a circle large enough to fit the bottom of the basin. Spread over a layer of mincemeat, then make another circle of dough to fit the basin. Continue in layers, ending with a top layer of dough. Cover securely and steam for 2½–3 hours.

Turn out on to a warm serving plate and serve very hot with Vanilla Custard or Lemon Sauce (see pages 35 and 81).

VARIATION
DE LA WARE PUDDING
Mix the mincemeat with 2 large cooking apples, cored, peeled and sliced.

COLLEGE PUDDING

Reputed to have been the first pudding boiled in a cloth, College Pudding was served to students in the college halls of Oxford and Cambridge as early as 1617.

85g (3oz) self-raising flour
1 teaspoon mixed spice
Pinch of salt
85g (3oz) fresh white or
     brown breadcrumbs
85g (3oz) shredded suet
85g (3oz) raisins
50g (1¾oz) currants
25g (1oz) chopped candied peel
50g (1¾oz) brown sugar
1 egg beaten
About 6 tablespoons milk

Serves 6

Well butter a 1.2 litre (2 pint) pudding basin. Sieve the flour, spice and salt together, then mix with all the dry ingredients in a mixing bowl. Add the beaten egg and enough milk to produce a soft dropping consistency. Spoon into the prepared basin, cover securely and steam for 2½ hours.

Turn out on to a warm plate and serve with Vanilla Custard, Lemon Sauce or a hard sauce (see pages 35, 81 and 55). As children we loved this pudding with a sprinkling of demerara sugar and a large lump of salted butter!

THE DUCHESS'S PUDDING

A light steamed almond-flavoured sponge pudding with chopped nuts, peel and dried fruit. I don't know which duchess inspired this pudding, but it is delicious and would make a lighter alternative to Christmas pudding.

115g (4oz) unsalted butter
115g (4oz) caster sugar
2 eggs
140g (5oz) self-raising flour
25g (1oz) raisins
25g (1oz) chopped glacé
  cherries
25g (1oz) chopped candied peel
25g (1oz) chopped walnuts
  or almonds
A few drops of almond essence
About 2 tablespoons water
  or milk

FOR THE LEMON OR
  ORANGE SAUCE
4 tablespoons homemade lemon
  or orange curd
150ml (¼ pint) single cream

Serves 6

Butter an 850ml (1½ pint) pudding basin. Cream the butter and sugar together until pale and fluffy. Beat the eggs and add gradually to the creamed mixture, beating well between each addition. Sieve the flour and fold gently into the mixture using a metal spoon. Add fruit, peel and nuts, almond essence and enough water or milk to give a soft dropping consistency. Put into the prepared basin, cover securely and steam for 1½–2 hours until firm and well risen. When cooked, turn the pudding on to a warm serving plate and serve hot with Vanilla Custard, Jam or Lemon Sauce (see pages 35, 67 and below).

LEMON OR ORANGE SAUCE
Mix lemon or orange curd and cream together. Heat in a saucepan over a low heat until hot but not boiling. Serve in a warmed jug.

RICH FIG AND ALMOND PUDDING

Figs are often associated with religious festivals, and fig pudding was traditionally eaten on Mothering Sunday in Lancashire. Further south in Buckinghamshire and the home counties, figs were eaten on Palm Sunday. This custom was said to be connected with the gospel account of the barren fig tree. The use of figs makes this a very substantial pudding for Christmas.

225g (8oz) dried figs
225g (8oz) stoned dates
115g (4oz) raisins
2 tablespoons brandy, rum
  or Madeira
225g (8oz) self-raising flour
Pinch of salt
175g (6oz) fresh white
  breadcrumbs
175g (6oz) suet
50g (1¾oz) ground almonds
3 eggs
Grated rind and juice of
  1 lemon
A little milk or water

Serves 6

Chop the figs and dates, mix with raisins and sprinkle with brandy, rum or Madeira. Cover and leave to soak for at least 1 hour. Butter a 1.2 litre (2 pint) pudding basin well. Sieve the flour and salt together into a mixing bowl. Stir in the crumbs, suet and ground almonds. Beat the eggs and mix into the dry ingredients with the lemon rind and juice. Add the fruit and mix thoroughly, adding a little milk or water if necessary, to make a soft dropping consistency. Turn into the prepared basin, cover securely and steam for 4 hours until firm and well risen. Serve hot with Vanilla Custard or a hard sauce (see pages 35 and 55) or with Eliza Acton's Madeira Sauce (see page 67) or clotted cream.

GRANNY'S LEG

Also known as Spotted Dog, this is a suet roly-poly pudding studded with currants — everybody's idea of a nursery treat. Until the end of the 19th century, it appeared as the first course of a meal to take the edge off the appetite, in the same way as Yorkshire Pudding used to be, and any left over was served with the vegetables and meat to make them go further.

175g (6oz) self-raising flour
Pinch of salt
85g (3oz) suet
50g (1¾oz) caster sugar
175g (6oz) currants
4–6 tablespoons milk

Serves 6

Sieve the flour and salt together into a mixing bowl. Stir in the suet, sugar and currants. Mix in sufficient milk to make a soft dough. Roll out on a floured board to an oblong shape about 20 x 30 cm (8 x 12in) and roll up like a Swiss roll. Wrap loosely in buttered and pleated greaseproof paper and then in pleated kitchen foil so that the pudding has room to expand to keep it light. Steam for 1½–2 hours in a large pan or fish kettle.

When cooked, unwrap the pudding, turn out on to a hot dish and serve very hot with Vanilla Custard Sauce (see page 35) or brown sugar and melted butter.

VARIATIONS
Mincemeat or golden syrup can be used instead of jam.

SHIRT-SLEEVE PUDDING OR SUETY JACK
Make the dough as before, omitting the currants. Roll out as before, then spread thickly with 175–225g (6–8oz) blackcurrant jam, leaving a 2.5cm (1in) border all the way round the edges. Brush these edges with milk and roll up evenly. Pinch the ends well to seal and keep in the jam. Cook as before and serve with Vanilla Custard Sauce (see page 35).

TRADITIONAL CHRISTMAS PLUM PUDDING

This heavy, rich pudding did not become associated with Christmas fare until the 19th century, when Prince Albert introduced it because he was so fond of it. It is traditional to bury a silver coin, if you have one, in the mixture. All the family should stir the pudding in turn on Stir-up Sunday, the Sunday before Advent, and make a wish at the same time. The coin should then be pushed in, plus a ring and a thimble; the coin is to bring worldly fortune, the ring a marriage and the thimble a life of blessedness.

225g (8oz) large prunes
300ml (½ pint) cold tea
225g (8oz) currants
225g (8oz) sultanas
225g (8oz) large raisins
225g (8oz) self-raising flour
¼ teaspoon salt
½ teaspoon baking powder
1 teaspoon mixed spice
½ teaspoon grated nutmeg
½ teaspoon cinnamon
½ teaspoon ground ginger
450g (1lb) fresh white
   breadcrumbs
225g (8oz) soft dark
   brown sugar
225g (8oz) shredded suet
50g (1¾oz) candied citron
   peel, chopped
50g (1¾oz) candied orange and
   lemon peel, finely chopped

Soak the prunes overnight in cold tea. Next day, drain, remove the stones and chop finely. The addition of prunes gives a richer, darker colour to the pudding as well as a very good flavour. Wash and dry all the remaining dried fruit and stone the raisins if necessary.

Sieve the flour, salt, baking powder and spices together into a very large bowl. Add breadcrumbs, sugar and suet, mixing in each ingredient thoroughly. Gradually mix in all the dried fruit, candied peel and almonds. Stir in the rind and juice of the lemon and orange, followed by the grated carrot and apple. Pour in the stout and mix until smooth. Cover a basin with a clean cloth and leave in a cool place overnight or longer if convenient (the flavour will improve). In fact, the mixture can be left to stand for a fortnight or longer at this point. Stir the mixture every day if you decide to do this.

On the day you want to cook the puddings, add the beaten eggs. Stir furiously until the pudding ingredients are thoroughly blended. Add enough rum to make a soft dropping consistency. Spoon the mixture into greased pudding basins to come within 2.5cm (1in) of the rim, packing the mixture down well with the back of a wooden spoon. You will need 5 x 450g (1lb) basins or 2 x 900g (2lb) and 1 x 450g (1lb) basin. Cover the top of each with greased greaseproof paper. Put a thick layer of flour on top of the greaseproof paper, pressing it down well (this will become a solid paste and act as a seal both for cooking and storing). Then cover with another piece of

115g (4oz) blanched almonds,
   chopped
Grated rind and juice of
   1 orange
Grated rind and juice of
   1 lemon
115g (4oz) carrot, grated
115g (4oz) cooking apple, grated
300ml (½ pint) stout
3 eggs, beaten
Rum to mix, about 4 tablespoons
Icing sugar, to sprinkle
Brandy, whisky, rum or kirsch to
   set alight

Makes 5 x 450g (1lb) puddings

greaseproof paper. Finally, cover the basins with a pudding cloth, muslin or aluminium foil, making a pleat in the centre to allow room for the puddings to rise during cooking. Tie securely with string and make a handle of string across the top of each basin, so that you can lift the puddings in and out of the pan easily.

Place the puddings in a steamer, double boiler, or in a large pan of gently boiling water. Steam for at least 6 hours, topping up the water level from time to time with boiling water. When cooked, remove the puddings from the pan and leave until cold. Renew the top piece of greaseproof paper and cloth and store in a cool, dry place until needed.

On the great day, steam again for 2–3 hours before serving. Turn out on to a large platter. Sprinkle with icing sugar. Heat some brandy, whisky, rum or Kirsch in a small saucepan or ladle. Pour over the pudding and set alight. Bring the pudding to the table, burning, and surrounded by a hedge of holly. Any spirit can be used, but you will find that rum burns longer. Make sure your holly doesn't go up in smoke!

SNOWDON PUDDING

This pudding was re-named after Prince Albert when he came over to England, but this caused a controversy, endangering the peace between England and Wales. It was said very unkindly that 'a bad Albert Pudding will make a good Snowdon Pudding'. However, the original pudding, named after the Welsh mountain, is much older and brought fame to the hotel at the foot of Snowdon where it was served to hungry climbers and walkers.

115g (4oz) raisins or sultanas
25g (1oz) chopped angelica
115g (4oz) fresh white
   breadcrumbs
25g (1oz) ground rice
   or rice flour
115g (4oz) suet
Pinch of salt
25g (1oz) brown sugar
Grated rind of 1 lemon
85g (3oz) lemon marmalade
2 eggs
3–4 tablespoons full-cream milk

Serves 6

Butter a 1.25 litre (2 pint) pudding basin thoroughly. Sprinkle 1 tablespoon raisins or sultanas and chopped angelica over the bottom of the buttered basin. Mix together the remaining raisins or sultanas with the dry ingredients and lemon rind. Stir in the marmalade. Beat the eggs and add to the mixture with enough milk to make a soft dropping consistency. Spoon carefully into the prepared basin. Cover securely, then steam for about 2 hours until well-risen.

Allow to shrink slightly before unmoulding on to a warm serving plate. Serve hot with Eliza Acton's Madeira Sauce or Lemon Sauce (see pages 67 and 81).

DATE AND WALNUT PUDDING

A very popular pudding from the early 19th century.

115g (4oz) roughly chopped
    dates
1 tablespoon rum
85g (3oz) self-raising flour
Pinch of salt
½ teaspoon mixed spice
85g (3oz) fresh white or brown
    breadcrumbs
85g (3oz) suet
2 heaped tablespoons soft
    brown sugar
50g (1¾oz) roughly chopped
    walnuts
2 eggs
1–2 tablespoons milk or water

Serves 6

Soak the chopped dates in the rum while you prepare the pudding. Butter thoroughly an 850ml (1½ pint) pudding basin.

Sieve the flour, salt and spice together into a bowl. Stir in the breadcrumbs, suet, sugar, chopped walnuts and dates, including the rum. Beat the eggs and add to the pudding mixture with enough milk to make a soft dropping consistency. Turn the pudding mixture into the prepared basin, cover securely and steam for about 2 hours.

Serve hot with a hard sauce (see page 55), Vanilla Custard Sauce (see page 35) or thick cream.

GOLDEN SYRUP SPONGE

Still everybody's favourite, this lovely pudding was made across the UK after golden syrup was first produced in the 19th century.

115g (4oz) butter
115g (4oz) caster sugar
2 eggs
115g (4oz) self-raising flour
Pinch of salt   1 tsp b. powder
1–2 tablespoons cold water
3 tablespoons golden syrup

Serves 6

Butter an 850ml (1½ pint) pudding basin thoroughly. Cream the butter and sugar together until pale and fluffy. Beat the eggs and add a little at a time to the creamed mixture, beating well between each addition. Sieve the flour and salt together and carefully fold into the mixture using a metal spoon. Add enough water to make a soft dropping consistency.

Spoon golden syrup into the buttered basin, then pour on the sponge mixture. Cover securely, then steam for 1½–2 hours until well risen and spongy.

Serve hot with Vanilla Custard, Lemon or Syrup Sauce (see pages 35, 81 and 94), or with clotted cream – particularly good for a summer dinner party in the garden.

VARIATIONS
MARMALADE OR JAM SPONGE
Replace the golden syrup with good-quality marmalade or jam. Serve with Jam or Marmalade Sauce (see pages 67 and 93).

GINGER SYRUP SPONGE
Sieve 1½ teaspoons ground ginger with the flour.

MY MOTHER'S GINGER PUD

I remember this lovely suety pudding from my childhood. My mother adapted a recipe dated 1905 and came up with this 'rib-sticker'. If you are very fond of ginger, try adding a small amount of chopped stem ginger to the mixture before cooking.

115g (4oz) self-raising flour
Pinch of salt
2 heaped teaspoons
    ground ginger
115g (4oz) fresh white
    breadcrumbs
115g (4oz) suet
2 heaped tablespoons
    golden syrup
1 level teaspoon bicarbonate
    of soda
3 tablespoons milk

FOR THE GINGER SAUCE
2 pieces preserved stem ginger
1 tablespoon caster sugar
1 tablespoon dark rum
150ml (¼ pint) double cream

Serves 6

Sieve the flour, salt and ginger together into a mixing bowl. Stir in the breadcrumbs and suet. Melt the syrup over a gentle heat until just runny. Dissolve the bicarbonate of soda in milk and add to the syrup. Pour into the dry ingredients and mix well. Turn into a greased 850ml (1½ pint) pudding basin. Cover securely and steam for 2–2½ hours until firm and well risen. Serve hot with Ginger Sauce (see below), Vanilla Custard or Syrup Sauce (see pages 35 and 94) or whipped or clotted cream.

GINGER SAUCE
Chop the ginger very finely. Mix with the sugar and rum. Stir in the double cream and continue stirring until thick. Chill before serving.

GUARD'S PUDDING

Originally known as Burbridge Pudding and said to be a favourite of the guards, hence its new name. It is a very traditional British steamed pudding, made with raspberry jam.

3 tablespoons good-quality
    raspberry jam
115g (4oz) butter
115g (4oz) soft brown sugar
115g (4oz) fresh brown
    breadcrumbs
2 eggs, beaten
Pinch of salt
Grated rind and juice of
    1 lemon
1 level teaspoon bicarbonate
    of soda

FOR THE RASPBERRY SAUCE
225g (8oz) fresh raspberries
85g (3oz) caster sugar
Juice of 1 lemon
2 tablespoons water

Serves 6

Butter a 1.2 litre (2 pint) pudding basin and put a large tablespoon of the jam in the bottom. Cream the butter and sugar together until fluffy, then blend in the remaining jam. Add the breadcrumbs, beaten eggs, salt and lemon rind. Dissolve the bicarbonate of soda in the lemon juice, then add to the mixture. Mix well and turn into the basin. Cover securely, then steam for 2½ hours until well risen and firm. Serve hot with Vanilla Custard Sauce (see page 35) or cream and Raspberry Sauce (see below).

RASPBERRY SAUCE

Heat all the ingredients in a saucepan over a very low heat. Simmer gently for 5 minutes. Rub through a sieve. Taste for sweetness.

MARMALADE PUDDING

An old-fashioned suet pudding from Mrs Beeton. Make sure you use a really good marmalade, preferably a home-made one.

115g (4oz) self-raising flour
Pinch of salt
115g (4oz) suet
115g (4oz) fresh white
    breadcrumbs
25g (1oz) soft brown sugar
175g (6oz) good-quality dark
    orange marmalade
Milk, to bind

Serves 4–6

Butter a 1.2 litre (2 pint) pudding basin. Sieve together the flour and salt into a bowl. Add the suet, breadcrumbs and sugar and mix well. Stir the marmalade really well into the dry ingredients, with just enough milk to make a fairly stiff dough. Pour into the prepared basin, cover securely and steam for 2½ hours. Turn out and serve with Vanilla Custard Sauce or Orange Cream Sauce (see pages 35 and 72).

RICH CABINET PUDDING WITH ORANGE SAUCE

Also called Charter Pudding, Chancellor's Pudding, Diplomatic Pudding, Newcastle Pudding or Ratafia Pudding. It is a rich custard dating back to the 19th century, when it was thickened with sponge cakes and ratafias and ornamented with glacé cherries and angelica. Cabinet Pudding is best made in a charlotte tin, but a 12.5cm (5in) cake tin or soufflé dish will do.

1 tablespoon brandy
1 teaspoon orange rind, grated
1 teaspoon candied orange peel
A little unsalted butter
A few natural glacé cherries
A little crystallized angelica
2 trifle sponges
25g (1oz) ratafia biscuits
600ml (1 pint) single cream
1 vanilla pod, split in half
6 eggs
1 tablespoon caster sugar
1 teaspoon cornflour

FOR THE ORANGE SAUCE
150ml (¼ pint) fresh orange juice
Caster sugar to taste
A little potato flour or arrowroot
½ teaspoon grated orange rind

Serves 6

Soak the grated orange rind and candied peel in the brandy. Grease a straight-sided charlotte mould or soufflé dish with the unsalted butter and line the bottom with buttered greaseproof paper or foil. Decorate the bottom with a few glacé cherry halves and angelica cut into diamond shapes. Cut the sponges into small squares and arrange over the candied fruit in the mould, with the ratafias crumbled into pieces on top.

Bring the cream and vanilla pod to the boil very slowly, then cool a little. Cream the eggs, sugar and cornflour together in a basin, then strain the cream on to the egg mixture, stirring vigorously. Add the soaked orange rind, peel and brandy to the custard, then pour carefully over the cake in the mould. Leave to soak for about 15 minutes, then cover tightly with foil and tie down with string. Steam gently for about 1 hour or until the custard is set and firm.

Meanwhile, make the sauce. Bring the orange juice and sugar to the boil. Mix a little potato flour or arrowroot in a tablespoon of cold water and stir this into the boiling juice a little at a time until you have the required consistency. Add the grated orange rind. Dust with caster sugar to prevent a skin forming. Serve the pudding hot with a little orange sauce.

SAUCES

150g (5½oz) caster sugar
100ml (3½fl oz) water
200ml (7fl oz) single cream
100g (3½oz) salted butter

CARAMEL SAUCE

Dissolve the sugar in the water in a saucepan. Do not stir. Put the pan on a moderate heat and let it bubble away until it reaches a rich amber colour. Add the cream and take off the heat. Whip in the butter and pour around a baked apple or over ice cream.
If you want it thicker, use double or whipping cream instead of single.

1 level teaspoon cornflour
Juice of 1 orange
300ml (½ pint) white wine
4 heaped tablespoons marmalade
2 tablespoons soft brown sugar

MARMALADE SAUCE

Dissolve the cornflour in the orange juice. Heat the wine, marmalade and sugar in a saucepan until the sugar has dissolved, stirring from time to time. Stir in the cornflour mixture and bring to the boil, stirring well. Simmer for 2 minutes. Serve hot.

15g (½oz) cornflour
300ml (½ pint) full-cream milk
Grated rind and juice of 1 lemon
Grated rind and juice of
  1 orange
3 tablespoons golden syrup

ORANGE AND LEMON SAUCE

Mix the cornflour to a paste with 3 tablespoons of the milk. Pour the remaining milk into a saucepan and heat gently. Add the lemon and orange rind. Pour the hot milk slowly on to the cornflour, stirring continuously. Return the sauce to the pan and simmer for 3 minutes, stirring gently. Stir in the fruit juices and golden syrup.

4 tablespoons golden syrup
2 tablespoons water
Juice of ½ lemon

SYRUP SAUCE

Simmer the syrup and water together in a small saucepan for 2–3 minutes. Add the lemon juice and serve hot.

4 tablespoons treacle or
   golden syrup
150ml (½ pint) single cream

TREACLE CREAM SAUCE

Melt the treacle or syrup in a small saucepan. Add the cream and heat until almost boiling. Serve hot.

60g (2oz) butter
150g (5½oz) demerara sugar
1 tablespoon golden syrup
150g (5½oz) evaporated milk

BUTTERSCOTCH SAUCE

Melt the butter, then add the sugar and syrup. Stir until dissolved, then pour in the evaporated milk. Turn up the heat and beat until boiling. Serve hot.

350ml (12fl oz) water
115g (4oz) caster sugar
1½ tablespoons cornflour
25g (1oz) cocoa powder
1 tablespoon instant
   coffee granules
50g (1¾oz) good-quality
   dark chocolate
2 strips of orange zest
Grand Marnier to taste

CHOCOLATE ORANGE SAUCE

This easy sauce can be stored in the refrigerator for 4 weeks to use on ice cream or any pudding whenever you fancy. Combine 200ml (7fl oz) water and the sugar in a saucepan. Bring to the boil, stirring occasionally to dissolve the sugar. In a bowl, mix the remaining water with the cornflour and cocoa powder. When the sugar syrup is boiling, stir the cocoa mixture again and then pour it into the pan. Whisk very well, then simmer for 5 minutes. Add the coffee, chocolate and orange zest and stir until smooth. Remove from the heat, cover and leave to cool completely. When the sauce is cold, strain it and flavour to taste with liqueur. Pour the sauce into a jar, cover and store in the refrigerator until needed.

115g (4oz) good-quality plain
    chocolate, broken into pieces
3 tablespoons strong black
    coffee
50g (1¾oz) unsalted butter

CHOCOLATE AND COFFEE SAUCE

Put the chocolate and coffee into the top of a double saucepan and stir over the heat until the chocolate has melted. Beat in the butter gradually until the sauce is smooth and glossy.

2 large egg yolks
1 tablespoon cornflour
200ml (7fl oz) cider
2 tablespoons muscovado sugar
½ teaspoon ground cinnamon
400ml (14fl oz) double cream

CIDER CUSTARD

In a small basin mix the egg yolks with the cornflour until smooth. Gradually add the cider, the sugar and the cinnamon. Pour into a saucepan and heat gently. Add the cream and whisk constantly over the heat until the custard has thickened.

425ml (¾ pint) double cream
40g (1½oz) caster sugar
2–3 tablespoons orange brandy
Grated rind of 1 orange

HOT BRANDIED CREAM

Put the ingredients into a small pan. Bring to the boil over a low heat, then simmer for 2 minutes. Serve with Christmas pudding.

115g (4oz) demerara sugar
2 tablespoons water
300ml (½ pint) strong black
    coffee
2 tablespoons Tia Maria

COFFEE SAUCE

Dissolve the sugar in the water by heating gently in a saucepan. When the sugar has dissolved, boil rapidly until the syrup becomes golden. Add the coffee and Tia Maria. Boil for a few minutes until syrupy.

INDEX

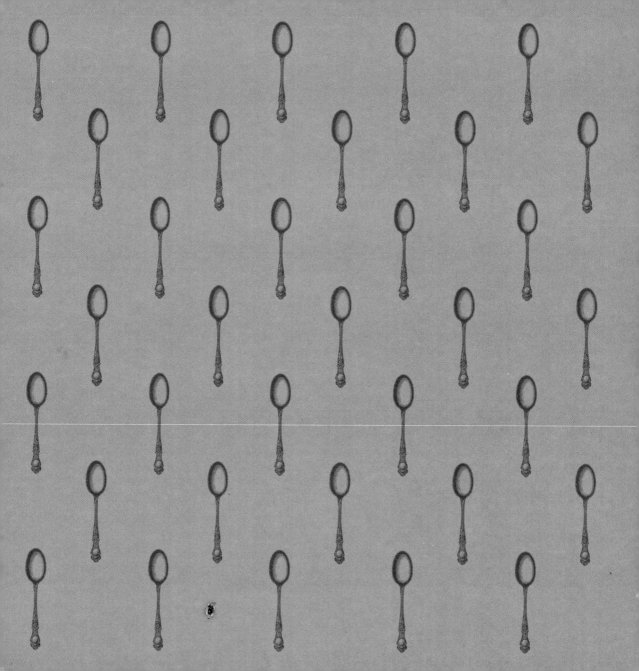